Themes in RE
Learning from Religions

2

Tracey Ellis and Joy White

Series Editor: Joe Jenkins

The publishers would like to thank Mohinder Singh Chahal of the Sikh Missionary Society, Harfiyah Haleem and colleagues at the IQRA Trust and Rasamandala Das of the Oxford Centre for Vishnu and Hindu Studies for their invaluable advice on the content of this publication.

Heinemann Educational Publishers
Halley Court, Jordan Hill, Oxford OX2 8EJ
a division of Reed Educational & Professional Publishing Ltd.
Heinemann is a registered trademark of Reed Educational and Professional Publishing Ltd.

OXFORD   MELBOURNE   AUCKLAND
JOHANNESBURG   BLANTYRE   GABORONE
IBADAN   PORTSMOUTH (NH) USA   CHICAGO

Text © Tracey Ellis and Joy White 2002
First published in 2002

06 05 04 03 02
10 9 8 7 6 5 4 3 2 1

British Library Cataloguing in Publication Data
A catalogue record for this book is available from the British Library

ISBN 0 435 30766 5

Produced by bigtop, Bicester
Original illustrations © Heinemann Educational Publishers, 2002
Illustrated by Jane Smith and Linda Scott.
Picture research by Jennifer Johnson
Printed and bound in Spain by Mateu Cromo

Acknowledgements

The publishers would like to thank the following for the use of copyright material: John Foster for the poems *Not the Answer* on p. 18; *'What makes you angry, Mum' I asked'* on p. 26; *The Day I became a vegetarian* on p. 52 © 1995 John Foster from *Standing on the Sidelines* (Oxford University Press) included by permission of the author; *Perspectives Winter 1998* for the extract on p. 21 © The Beth Shalom Holocaust Centre, Nottinghamshire; © HarperCollins Publishers Ltd for the extract from *The Scroll The Tabloid Bible* by Nick Page; *Looking for Space* words and music by John Denver © 1975 Cherry Lane Music Publishing Company, Inc (ASCAP) and Dreamworks Songs (ASCAP). Worldwide rights for Dreamworks songs administered by Cherry Lane Music Publishing Company, Inc. international copyright secured. All Rights Reserved, for the lyrics on p. 50.

The publishers would like to thank the following for permission to use photographs:
Sally & Richard Greenhill/Richard Greenhill p.4; TRIP/H Rogers p. 7; Camera Press/Lynn Pelham p. 9; Empics/Tony Marshall p. 10; TRIP/H Rogers p. 15; The Holocaust Centre/David Brown p. 21; TRIP/G Hopkinson p. 22 (upper left); Salvation Army/Gary Freeman p. 22 (upper centre); Andes Press Agency/Carlos Reyes-Manzo p. 22 (upper right); Karuna Trust p. 22 (lower left); Format Photographers/Ulrike Preuss p. 22 (lower right); TRIP /H Rogers p. 25; Bridgeman Art Library/Giraudon p. 27; Camera Press/David Dyson p. 28; Kobal Collection/Columbia p. 32 (left); Kobal Collection p. 32 (right); Camera Press p. 34; Camera Press/Brian Snyder p. 36; Angela Hampton p. 46; TRIP/ Z Harasym p. 48 (upper left); Empics/Adam Davy p. 48 (upper centre); Photofusion (Phillip Carr) p. 48 (upper right); Sally & Richard Greenhill/Sally Greenhill p. 48 (lower); TRIP/H Rogers p. 50 Panos Pictures/Roderick Johnson; p. 55; The Frick Collection, New York p. 63; TRIP/A Tovy p. 66; Collections/Loz Simpson p. 69 (left); Andes Press Agency/Carlos Reyes-Manzo p. 69 (right); Science Photo Library/US National Archives p. 70; Robert Harding Picture Library/Christopher Rennie p. 71; Sally & Richard Greenhill/Sally Greenhill p. 74 (left); Camera Press p. 74 (right); Panos Pictures/Trevor Page p. 78 (left); Panos Pictures/Giacomo Pirozzi p. 78 (right); TRIP/H Luther p. 79 (left); TRIP/H Rogers p. 79 (upper right); TRIP/ H Rogers p. 79 (lower right); TRIP/H Rogers p. 81; Photofusion/David Hoffman p. 86.

Cover photograph by Andes Press Agency/Carlos Reyes-Manzo (Dalai Lama); Panos Pictures/Marc French (Buddhists praying); Format photographers/ Melanie Friend (woman lighting candle).

The publishers have made every effort to trace copyright holders, but if they have inadvertently overlooked any they will be pleased to make the necessary arrangements at the first opportunity.

Websites
Links to appropriate websites are given throughout the book. Although these were up to date at the time of writing, it is essential for teachers to preview these sites before using them with pupils. This will ensure that the web address (URL) is still accurate and the content is suitable for your needs.

We suggest that you bookmark useful sites and consider enabling pupils to access them through the school intranet. We are bringing this to your attention as we are aware of legitimate sites being appropriated illegally by people wanting to distribute unsuitable or offensive material. We strongly advise you to purchase suitable screening software so that pupils are protected from unsuitable sites and their material.

If you do find that the links given no longer work, or the content is unsuitable, please let us know. Details of changes will be posted on our website.

Contents

The meaning of relationships

In this chapter you will consider the relationships you have with different people and you will think about your relationship with yourself by focusing on Christianity, Buddhism, Sikhism and Judaism.

What is a relationship? When we think about having a relationship with someone, what do we mean by this? Do we mean someone we are close to? Someone who cares about us? Someone we smile at as we pass on the street?

We are all sons or daughters; many of us are brothers or sisters. We all know what it is like to be a pupil in school! And we all have relationships from the moment we are born.

Activity

1 Produce a spider diagram to show all the people you have a relationship with.

- Are these relationships all the same?
- Share your thoughts with a partner.

Relationships are funny things! They are never straightforward or easy. Sometimes they can make us feel happy and safe; sometimes they can make us feel sad and lonely.

If you think about your relationships with your friends, you have fun with them, share interests, secrets and thoughts, and sit next to them in class. These are all the good things about being together, but then come the bad things too! Friends fall out with each other, say things that can hurt feelings and they can be moody.

2 Take one example of someone you have a relationship with. Make a list of all the things that make that relationship a good one.

3 Make a list of the things that can happen that can hurt and upset you.

We all have a relationship with our friends

Activity

1 Just because something in a relationship can cause you to feel angry or upset, does this mean the relationship should end? Or do we need to forgive and forget? What do you think the term 'forgiveness' means? Is this always easy?
Discuss these questions with a partner.

2 Forgiveness is not always easy, but it is important. If people do not forgive, then they can hold grudges. Imagine for a moment what your life would be like if people did not forgive you for the things you have done wrong. Share your thoughts with a partner.

Forgiveness

Forgiveness was something Jesus taught people about through stories. One **parable** in particular deals with the issue of forgiveness. It is the Parable of the Prodigal Son.

In this story, Ben asked his father for his **inheritance** money early. He took the money and went off to the bright lights of the city, where he spent his money in the casinos, attracting the attention of various people who were happy to have him pick up their bills. He had a great time; the gambling and the fast life suited him down to the ground. But, as we all know, money does not grow on trees, and he soon ran out of cash. As the money ran out, so did his friends. They did not want to hang around with someone who could not pay their bills. Ben was left penniless and friendless. He had cut off all ties with his family and was alone.

Sad and lonely, he tried to get a job, but was completely unqualified for anything except farm work. Being desperate, he had to take work looking after pigs. The farmer he worked for was nothing like his dad; he was mean and unfriendly, forcing Ben to live and eat with the pigs. This, of course, was nothing like the life Ben had been used to and it made him feel sadder than ever. He decided to go back to his dad and ask him to give him a job. He knew that his behaviour had caused pain and upset and that he no longer deserved to be called a son.

What do you think happens next?

If you were Ben's father what would you do? Why?

Ben's dad actually welcomed his son back home; he was delighted to see him and threw a party to celebrate. Why do you think he did this?

In this story Jesus was trying to show that we should forgive people because we love them, and so that we can move on from hurt and anger. In the parable, who do you think the father represents, and who does Ben represent?

Activity

Further activity

People do not always say what they mean when it comes to relationships with other people. Often we get embarrassed at having to say 'thank you', 'sorry' or 'I love you!'
Why do people get embarrassed? Do you find these things easy?
Thinking about this idea, if you had to say one thing to your parents, teacher or a friend, what would it be? Jot down your thoughts on this.

Thought diary

You have been thinking about whom you have relationships with in this unit. Jot down one or two reasons why you think relationships are an important part of life.

Key Words

Inheritance – *Money you are left in someone's will.*
Parable – *A story with a special meaning.*

Marriage as a relationship

Relationships can be complicated and involve lots of emotions. When you are married the relationship becomes even more complex because trust and honesty become more important.

Activity

1 In small groups, make a list of characters in soap operas who are married. Do you think their marriages will last forever? Why? Why not?
Based on your thoughts, try to compile a list of ingredients necessary for a successful marriage.

2 Unfortunately, some relationships break down and end. Marriage is an example of a relationship that does not always last for ever. Based on your discussions, produce a spider diagram showing the different reasons why marriages break down.

3 Some people believe that when we are young we do not always know who our ideal husband or wife would be. They believe that parents can be better judges of character. So some people choose to have an **arranged marriage**, where their parents help them to decide who they should marry. In these instances, parents look for things other than just someone who is attractive.

Make a list of things parents might think are important when considering a marriage partner for their son or daughter.

4 Some parents might advertise for a suitable partner for their child. Imagine your parents are advertising for a partner for you. What might they say about you, and what would they look for in a perfect partner for you?

5 Do you think people should marry for love? Can you think of any reasons why some parents might not think this is a good idea?

6 Muhammad (pbuh), the prophet of Islam, said:

> *A woman may be married for four qualifications: for her wealth, her birth, her beauty or her religion. So choose the religious one.*
>
> The Hadith

Why do you think Muhammad (pbuh) thought religion was a good reason to marry a woman?

Rama and Sita

The **Ramayana**, one of the great Hindu epics, tells the story of a married couple – Rama (an **avatar** of Vishnu) and his wife, Sita. It details all the things that happened to them in their married life; how they stayed true to each other when other people tried to split them up and how good battled against evil and won.

Rama and his wife Sita

The following is one example of an adventure Rama and Sita experienced.

Ravana was an evil king and he kidnapped Sita. Rama and his brother Lakshmana, along with Hanuman, the monkey warrior, set out to look for Sita. Along the way they had to face many difficult challenges. They set out across the sea and arrived in what is today called Sri Lanka.

Ravana was waiting for them with his army. Rama, his friends and army fought long and hard against Ravana and his men. The battle was difficult, but eventually Rama and his army beat Ravana, destroying him.

Rama rescued Sita and he wanted to prove to the world that his wife had been faithful to him during their long separation. To do this, Sita lit a fire and stepped into it. When she stepped out of it unhurt, everyone knew that she had been true to Rama.

Activity

Further activity

1 In pairs, imagine you are a married couple like Rama and Sita. Rama has just rescued his beautiful wife. What might their first conversation involve? What do you think they would they say to each other? Think about all the things Rama went through to rescue his wife, and why he did this.

RESEARCH:

2 Find out about wedding ceremonies from other cultures. What vows are made?

3 If you were to marry, what vows would you make?

Thought diary

In this unit you have seen that in Hinduism and in Islam arranged marriages take place. If you were to get married, would you allow your parents to help you choose a husband or wife? Explain your views.

Key Words

Arranged marriage – *A marriage where your parents help you choose your partner.*

Avatar – *An incarnation of the Hindu god Vishnu.*

Ramayana – *Holy book in Hinduism that tells of the adventures of Rama and Sita.*

Treating people differently

We all have times when things happen and we feel unhappy. Sometimes these things are caused by someone being cruel and unkind; sometimes it is because of things that are happening in the world.

One problem that has existed for a very long time, and something that still exists today, is prejudice. The word prejudice is two words joined together, 'pre' and 'judge'. The word itself means pre-judging someone, making judgements about someone when you do not even know them.

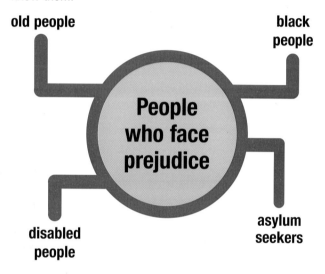

old people

black people

People who face prejudice

disabled people

asylum seekers

Activity

1 With a partner, think about all the different groups of people who suffer because other people make judgements about them and treat them differently.

  a Produce a spider diagram like the one in the picture above to show your thoughts.

  b Why are these people victims of prejudice? Why do you think they are treated differently?

  c Give an example to show how these people are victims of prejudice.

2 Make a list of words we could use to describe how victims of prejudice might feel.

3 Based on your thinking about prejudice, with a partner or in a small group act out a situation where someone is treated differently. Then discuss how you felt in the roles you played.

Prejudice is unacceptable in today's society. Everyone is equal and everyone is different, but no one is any better than anyone else. Yet people today suffer name-calling, threats, even death, because of prejudice. There have been famous cases where people have been killed because of the colour of their skin. Stephen Lawrence, a black British teenager, was one such example. He was stabbed in 1993 whilst waiting at a bus stop. No one yet has been found guilty of his murder.

Activity

In 1849 Benjamin Disraeli, the British Prime Minister, said:

*The difference of race is one of the reasons why I fear war may always exist; because race implies difference, difference implies **superiority**, and superiority leads to **predominance**.*

Working in pairs or small groups, discuss these questions, jot down your thoughts and share them with the class.

a Why do some people believe that they are better than others?

b How do you think we can teach people to stop being prejudiced?

In the 1960s in America, black people were victims of **discrimination**. They were treated differently because of the colour of their skin – regarded as second-class citizens and as servants for white people. Any black person who travelled on a bus had to sit at the back and give up their seat if a white person wanted to sit down.

Can you imagine living in that kind of society? How would you feel if you were treated like this?

Martin Luther King

One man who thought this was **intolerable** was **Martin Luther King**. He was born in America in 1929 and believed that everyone had the right to be treated equally. Everyone had been created by God and therefore everyone was equal. For him, something had to change and he organized marches and peaceful protests. The blacks **boycotted** the buses and did not give in until they were given equal rights.

Martin Luther King believed that the only way to stop prejudice was to use non-violent methods of protest. For him, fighting and guns would not solve a problem – they would only make it worse. He was very powerful and successful and he did not throw a punch.

Martin Luther King was shot dead in 1968.

His son, Martin Luther King Jr, said:

When evil men plot, good men must plan. When evil men shout ugly words of hatred, good men must commit themselves to the glories of love.

Jesus said that when faced with difficult situations we should not retaliate with violence. His advice was that we should:

*Not return hate with hate.
Turn the other cheek.
Love your neighbour.*

Jesus lived his life using love as his guide. This love was called **agape**. It meant that whenever he had to make a decision he thought about what was the most caring thing to do. Sometimes this meant he had to mix with people who were unpopular, like **lepers**, Samaritans and prostitutes.

Activity

Further activity

Do you think we should live our lives thinking about helping each other and acting toward each other with love?

If we did this, would the world be a better place? Explain your answer.

Thought diary

Franklin D Roosevelt, an American President (1882–1945) said:

> *If civilization is to survive, we must **cultivate** the science of human relationships – the ability of all peoples, of all kinds, to live together, in the same world at peace.*

How can we get people to take this idea on board and act on it?

Jot down your thoughts on this question.

Key Words

Agape – *Christian love meaning care and compassion. This belief is also central to other world faiths.*

Boycot – *To refuse to use something.*

Cultivate – *Improve, help the growth and development of anything.*

Discrimination – *Treated differently because of prejudice.*

Franklin D Roosevelt (1882–1945) – *American President in the 1940s.*

Intolerable – *Unacceptable.*

Leper – *Someone who suffers from a skin disease called leprosy.*

Martin Luther King (1929–68) – *An African-American civil rights leader who believed that all people should be treated equally.*

Predominance – *Having more power.*

Superiority – *Being better than someone else.*

How can we achieve success?

Football – a team sport

Relationships work best when we all work together as a team. Football teams are most successful when each player plays his very best and works with the other members of his team.

There are many occasions where people have worked together focusing on a common goal rather than thinking about their differences.

Often the news will report stories of people of different religions who do not **co-operate**, sometimes with disastrous consequences. All too often we see images of war because people of different faiths are opposed to each other rather than working together and co-operating.

Fortunately, there are also stories about people co-operating, working together to achieve success. One such example tells of how a Sikh man helped the **Dalai Lama**, the spiritual leader of Tibetan Buddhism, to escape the Chinese army. Tibet is a large country that borders with China. It is a land rich in resources and with a small population. The Tibetan people grew their own food and enjoyed a simple life. Their young leader was the Dalai Lama, a man admired and respected by the people. He was hugely influential amongst the people of Tibet.

In 1959, the Chinese army invaded Tibet and put the life of the Dalai Lama at risk. He knew he had to get to India if he was to survive.

In India, a man named Harmander Singh was given the task of making sure the Dalai Lama made it to safety. He knew the risks involved in his mission but, with his men, was prepared to help. They met the Dalai Lama at the border between Tibet and India.

A Buddhist custom is to give someone a scarf when you meet. Knowing this, Harmander Singh had come prepared with a scarf to give to the Dalai Lama. The two men exchanged scarves and rested before continuing their journey.

Harmander Singh took his responsibilities seriously, guarding the Dalai Lama at night and riding alongside him during the day. He delivered him to safety and returned home.

Soon afterwards, many other Buddhists fled Tibet, fearing for their lives. On their journey to safety, many were injured. Harmander Singh did all he could to take care of these people who were suffering as a result of persecution.

For his kindness and bravery he was awarded the Padma Shiri, an award given by the Indian Government for outstanding achievements.

Activity

Imagine you are Harmander Singh and you are keeping a diary as you help the Dalai Lama. What would you write? How would you feel about what was happening in Tibet?

The world: a perfect place?

Each time we turn on the news or open a newspaper we are faced with bad news of some kind or another: people who have died, bombs that have gone off and children starving to death. This is the world we live in – a world where death and destruction is a part of everyday life for many people.

Schools cash crisis

WOMAN FIGHTS FOR RIGHT TO DIE

BABY FOUND ON THE MOORS

More dying from hunger

Activity

Further activity

1 With a partner, choose a problem from one of the headlines on the left or one you think needs to be resolved in the world. Explain how you think we should deal with the problem. Why? Is your thinking based on the idea we should treat people equally, or that we should share?
Is it based on something else?

Be prepared to present your thoughts to others in the class.

2 Philosopher St Augustine (354–430 AD) said:

> *Hear the other side*

Why are these words considered to be wise?

3 Imagine you work for an advertising company and you have to advertise the world we live in as the perfect place for people from another planet to move to. Working either in pairs or small groups, design a poster that shows just how wonderful our world could be.

Thought diary

If you were to pass on words of wisdom to younger children about how problems in the world should be solved, what would your advice be? Make a list of 'do's' and 'don'ts'.

Key Words

Co-operate – *Work together as a team to achieve a common goal.*

Dalai Lama – *The spiritual and temporal leader of Tibetan Buddhism, who escaped from Tibet and now lives in exile in India.*

The relationship with myself

We have relationships with lots of people, but one of the most important relationships we have is with ourselves. If we do not feel happy with the person we are, then how well can we deal with other people and life itself? We need to be happy with ourselves in order to really enjoy life.

Confucius, a Chinese philosopher wrote:

> *To put the world right in order we must first put the nation in order; to put the nation in order, we must first put the family in order; to put the family in order, we must first cultivate our personal life; we must first set our hearts right.*

Activity

1 What do you think Confucius was saying about the world?

2 He lived between 551–479 BCE. Have we learnt anything in the last 2,500 years about how to get along with people?

3 a Snow White's wicked stepmother had a mirror that would tell her the truth about who was the fairest of them all. In the Harry Potter books, there was the mirror of Erised that revealed your heart's desires. If you were to look into a mirror, what would it tell you about the person you are?

b Draw two mirrors and, in one, either write words or draw sketches that show the good things that you have done.

In the other, draw or write the words that describe some of the bad things you have done.

What could you do to improve the person you are? Do you need any help to improve – if so, from whom?

Lots of people have things happen to them that make them realize that they need to make a change in their lives. Read the following story from Sikhism.

Guru Nanak Dev Ji, the first **Guru** in Sikhism, was travelling in Lahore in Pakistan and met with a banker who was very wealthy and greedy. The banker lived in a beautiful house surrounded by jewels and possessions. He invited Guru Nanak to his house for dinner and spent lots of money providing a sumptuous feast in his honour.

Guru Nanak attended the dinner and enjoyed the food, but realized that the banker needed to learn an important lesson. The banker asked Guru Nanak if there was anything he could do for him. 'I am very rich and very powerful – I can do anything you like!'

Guru Nanak thought for a while and then gave the banker a needle and asked him to look after it until they met again in the next world.

The banker was delighted to be given such an honour. He was very proud and showed the needle to his wife. She laughed out loud at her husband's stupidity. 'How are you going to take the needle with you into the next world?' she asked.

The banker then ran after Guru Nanak and asked him how he was to get the needle into the next world. Guru Nanak took pity on the banker and said to him, 'If you can't get the needle into the next world, how will you get all your possessions in?'

The banker suddenly realized what he was being taught. He made a decision to use his wealth and power to help those in need.

Thought diary

You have been thinking about people, their characters and how it can affect their personal life. Do you think people sometimes forget what is important in life and become focused on material possessions? Jot down some thoughts on this question.

Activity

Further activity

1 If you were the banker in Lahore, would you have given away your money? Explain your views.

2 Is the lesson being taught by Guru Nanak one that people today need to learn? Explain your thoughts.

3 Number the following characteristics in order of importance:

- Honesty
- Willingness to share
- Unselfishness
- Trustworthyness
- Goodness
- Kindness
- Thoughtfulness
- Courage

a How did you decide which characteristic was most important? Now share your list with a partner and try to combine your two lists into one.

b If you had to choose one of these characteristics that you think you have, which would you choose and why?

c If you had to choose one of these characteristics that you think you would like to have, which would you choose and why?

Those who love God, love everybody

4 Guru Nanak said this in the **Guru Granth Sahib Ji**. If people were to love everyone do you think the world would be a better place? How would it be improved? Share your answers with a partner.

Key Words

Guru – *The word means 'teacher'.*
Guru Granth Sahib Ji – *The holy book of Sikhism.*
Guru Nanak Dev Ji – *The first Guru in Sikhism.*

Relationships with God

Most religious people have a personal relationship with God. They believe that God listens to them and watches over them, looking after them and helping in times of need. This belief means that people communicate with their God.

Can you think of any ways in which people communicate with God?

You see, God, it's like this...

Activity

Many people pray to God. Can you think of any reasons why people pray? Share your ideas with a partner.

Some religious people think prayer is very important because it helps to remind people about their beliefs and stops them giving in to the temptation to do the wrong thing.

Muslims believe in Allah, and pray to Him five times a day. These daily prayers are one of the **five pillars**, their five key practices. Prayer in Islam is known as **salah** and is very important.

Before Muslims pray they have to prepare themselves. This preparation involves a wash. This wash is not the same as when you have a shower before school, where you wash your hair and use shower gel. It is a wash or shower that is completed to **symbolize** being clean and ready to face Allah. The ritual wash is known as **wudu**.

Muslims believe that when they pray they have to focus completely on Allah – they should not be thinking about anything else. They have to pray with the right intention or **niyyah**. Why do you think Muslims consider these things to be important when praying?

Muslims all around the world pray five times a day and they all face toward the holy city of Makkah. Makkah is considered holy to Muslims because it is the place where the first building was built for the worship of one God. This building is known as the **Ka'bah**. The Qur'an tells how the Prophet Ibrahim (Abraham) and his son Isma'il (Ishmael) built up its foundations and prayed to Allah that He would keep it holy.

What feelings do you think Muslims might feel knowing that Muslims all over the world are praying at the same time?

When Muslims pray, their bodies move through a set of positions: standing, bowing, sitting and **prostrating**. These positions, especially bowing and prostrating, help Muslims feel humble before Allah. These are called the **rak'ahs**.

Are there any other actions you know people perform when they pray? (They may be Muslim, or from another religion, for example, hands together, using rosary beads.) Can these things help people when they pray?

Lots of people learn to pray when they are very young. Have you ever prayed, perhaps when you were at junior school? Why did you pray? Was it a prayer you learned by heart? Were your prayers answered? Can you pray without believing in God?

Muslims at prayer

Activity

Further activity

Muslims can pray to Allah at any time in the day using **Du'a** prayers. Praying at these times might involve asking Allah for help, saying thank you for something, or asking for forgiveness.

If you were to pray and had to say thank you for something, what would you say thank you for and why?

Think carefully about all the things you are thankful for – you might need to make a list! If you think about other people in the world that are not as fortunate as you, it might help you to make your list.

Using a clean page present your thoughts either as a prayer or a letter using pictures to illustrate.

Thought diary

You have been thinking about prayer in this unit. Some people pray to God. Think quietly about your life and all the things that are happening: if you were to pray what would you say? Would you ask for help in making decisions? Would you say thank you? Would you say sorry? Would you ask for some strength to face a difficult situation?

Write down your thoughts.

Key Words

Du'a – *Personal prayers said by Muslims.*

Five Pillars – *Acts of worship which form the basis of everyday life for Muslims.*

Ka'bah – *The cube-shaped building in Makkah.*

Niyyah – *Right intention.*

Prostrate – *To place the face on the ground while kneeling.*

Rak'ahs – *The prayer cycle.*

Salah – *Second pillar of Islam, praying five times a day.*

Symbolize – *To represent something.*

Wudu – *Ritual washing before prayer.*

Assessment

In this chapter we have begun to think about relationships – how we deal with other people and with God. We have learned that there are many aspects to a relationship, both positive and negative, and that there are many different types of relationships too.

Here are a few questions that you might have thought about in each unit:

❶ *The meaning of relationships – What does it mean to have a relationship?*

❷ *Marriage as a relationship – Do you think people should have marriages arranged for them?*

❸ *Treating people differently – Why do you think people are prejudiced against others?*

❹ *How can we achieve success? – Is it better to achieve goals on your own or as part of a team?*

❺ *The relationship with myself – How can we be happy with ourselves?*

❻ *Relationships with God – In what ways do people communicate with God?*

Draw a spider diagram to show all the people you have relationships with at school and why they are important.

Reflecting on your progress

❶ To help you reflect on what you have learnt from this chapter, look back on your work, or in your Thought diary, and write a few lines on each of the following areas, giving reasons to improve your answers:

ⓐ What I enjoyed. Why?
ⓑ What I found difficult. Why?

❷ Pick an idea that you had and try to explain it clearly to another person. Think about:

- Where the idea came from.
- What the idea is about.
- Why you like the idea.
- The *best* way to explain it to someone.

❸ In your Thought diary, copy down five **skills** that you have used most during this chapter from the following list:

- I listened well to others.
- I gave reasons for my views.
- I expressed myself clearly.
- I tried to imagine other people's points of view.
- I developed my writing and artistic skills.
- I investigated a new topic by myself.
- I kept on task well.
- I used lots of imagination.
- I cared about the feelings of other people.
- I gave justified views.

❹ What facts did you learn? What do you understand now that you did not know about before? Make a spider diagram or a poster to show your thoughts.

Test yourself

❶ *Give an example of individual people or groups who suffer as a result of prejudice. Explain how they suffer. [Level 3 – AT1]*

❷ *How should people be treated? Explain your thoughts and include some religious teachings in your answer. [Level 4 – AT2]*

❸ *Think about people's relationships with God. What do you think are the benefits of having a relationship with God? [Level 6 – AT2]*

❹ *From all the religious teachings and stories you have looked at in this chapter, which do you think is the most important? Explain your thinking. [Level 6 – AT2]*

❺ *You have considered lots of different relationships in this chapter. What relationship do you consider to be the most precious one in your life? Give reasons for your answer. [Level 5 – AT2]*

What next?

❶ *Look at the list of skills opposite. Choose two that you want to improve on in the future. Perhaps you could note them down in your Thought diary. (Describe two ways in which you could improve them. Is there someone who could give you suggestions? Is there some way of reminding yourself of your aims in future lessons?)*

❷ *Think about the topic you enjoyed most. What could you do to investigate it further? Are there any websites or books that could help you find out more?*

Well done!

You know more, have thought more and improved your skills.
KEEP GOING! ✓

Standing by

Why is it
That when there's a fight
In the playground,
Everyone gathers round
And starts taking sides,
Even though most of them
Don't know who started it
Or what it's about?

Why is it
That when there's a fight
In the playground,
I join the others
And race to watch and cheer,
Even though I know
Deep down inside
Fighting's not the answer?

Extract from *Not the Answer*, from *Standing on the Sidelines* by John Foster

In this chapter you will consider why people stand by when they know something wrong is happening and explore how a person's religious beliefs might influence their actions by looking at Judaism, Christianity, Sikhism and Islam.

So, why is it? We often see something in school, on the streets, or even in our home, which deep down inside we know is wrong, but we do nothing about it.

Activity

We do not know why the people in the poem were fighting. Often when we are witnessing a happening we do not know the full story or we may react differently. How would you react in each of the following cases? (In your descriptions you should say why you chose to react in that particular way).

- The fight started because two boys were fighting over the same girlfriend.
- The fight started because one boy who is in Year 11 wanted money from the Year 7 pupil.
- The fight started because one boy called the other boy racist names.
- One of the boys has a knife.

The poem talks about a feeling 'deep down inside'. People often call this feeling their **conscience**. A conscience is a sense of right and wrong. Some people would say we have a natural sense of what is wrong. Other people would say we learn it through our life experiences.

Activity

Further activity

Many Christians consider their conscience as the voice of God within the **soul** which guides their daily life.

How do you think you have learnt what is right and wrong? Put the following in rank order.

- family?
- religious teachings and teachers?
- friends?
- own experiences?
- television?

Put the features that influence your life now in rank order, rank them as you think they might be in your life twenty years from now.

Pearl S. Buck wrote:

You cannot make yourself feel something you do not feel, but you can make yourself do right in spite of your feelings.

Pearl S. Buck

Can you remember a time when you did right in spite of your feelings?

Thought diary

Has there ever been a time in your life when you have stood by and watched someone being hurt.

Key Words

Conscience – *A sense of right and wrong especially in relation to a persons own actions and motives.*

Soul – *Part of human nature that is not just physical. The part which, some people believe, allows people to relate to God.*

Bystanding

Imagine you are sitting watching the television and no one is at home when SMASH! your bedroom window is broken. You run upstairs and there is a brick lying in the middle of the floor. Outside you can hear people laughing and shouting. CRASH! Now a window downstairs has been broken. There is no one home but you.

Activity

1 Make a list of those people who you would contact to help you. As well as friends and family, think about people whom you would consider it their duty to help.

2 Now imagine that groups of people night after night were coming to your house breaking windows, spraying graffiti on your door and shouting at you. Your family are now scared to go out. Who are you going to contact? Think of three people or groups of people who you will tell and who you expect to help you.

There are many people who we know would help because they are our family and friends. There are also many other people we would expect to help because that is their job and their duty. But imagine how you would feel if they decided it was not their business – if they were to become bystanders to watch what was happening.

In the 1930s there were many anti-Jewish laws passed through Germany. This happened over ten years so it was difficult to realize how bad things were getting.

JEWS NO LONGER ALLOWED TO ATTEND PLAYS OR FILMS

Jewish children no longer allowed to go to the same schools as other German children

JEWS MADE TO WEAR YELLOW STAR

JEWS NO LONGER ALLOWED TO GO TO SWIMMING POOLS OR SPORTS GROUNDS

JEWS FORBIDDEN TO KEEP ANY PETS

Jews no longer allowed to have telephones, bikes or ride in cars

We should never forget that everything Adolf Hitler did in Germany was 'legal'. Even so, I am sure that, had I lived in Germany at the time, I would have aided and comforted my Jewish brothers and sisters.

Martin Luther King Jr

The American religious leader Martin Luther King showed that as a Christian it would have been his duty to get involved.

Many Jews found that people who had been their friends now made the choice to ignore what was happening to them. The Jews felt **betrayed**. Some people thought that because they were not Jewish they should not get involved.

Lisa Vincent was a young Jewish girl who managed to escape to England just before the war but six other members of her family died.

During one dreadful night in Germany when many Jews were taken from their beds and their homes and businesses set alight, men and some women (including Lisa's mother) were taken separately away. Lisa was terrified as she was separated from the only family member she had left. Then she saw her school-friend, Wolfgang.

Lisa Vincent

She later wrote:

Of all the things which happened that night, perhaps what most sticks in my mind is the moment I looked at Wolfgang and he didn't look at me. And I thought, gosh, a friendly face! It was Wolfgang, and I knew him and he – nothing, just stone. He just didn't look. He knew it was me: he had seen me. He had to guard the flat and I didn't matter as a human being any more, I wasn't Lisa any more.

Activity

Further activity

1 What do you think Lisa meant when she says 'I wasn't Lisa any more'?

2 Do you think there might have been a difference between what Wolfgang's conscience was telling him to do and what he actually did?

3 Look through a newspaper. Are there any examples of situations where people were bystanders? Bring your findings back to the next lesson.

4 Imagine you had to show someone who speaks no English what the word 'bystander' means. In small groups, create a storyboard.

Thought diary

Make a note of a time when you have felt people let you down or betrayed you. Try to remember the emotions you felt and write them down.

Key Words

Betray – *To be false or disloyal.*
Legal – *Allowed by law.*

Actions speak louder than words

There are so many people who need our help. It could be friends, family or even strangers.

How often do we consider that the only way to help is to give money? Sometimes people give a few pounds to **charity** and feel they have done all they can do. There are so many ways we can help, ways that do not cost money but do cost thought and time.

Giving offerings of food – Hare Krishna

Helping the homeless

Donating clothes

Donating money to the Karuna Trust

Carer supporting an elderly resident at Nightingale House

Activity

1 Try to remember the last time you needed some help. Think about the actions that were taken to help you.

2 Discuss each of the following situations with a partner. Create a spider diagram of the many ways that the person could be helped.

- A neighbour whose husband has recently died.
- A friend who is off school ill for a month.

Helping others does not mean just helping your best friends and family.

In Jesus' time the Jews and Samaritans were often enemies. When Jesus told the **parable** of the Good Samaritan listeners would be surprised that it was a Samaritan who helped a Jew.

All religions teach that it is important to help other people. Although they realize that giving money to charity is an important way of helping, they also believe that there are many different ways they put their beliefs into practice.

Jesus said: 'I was hungry and you fed me, thirsty and you gave me a drink; I was a stranger and you received me in your homes, naked and you clothed me; I was sick and you took care of me… Whenever you did this for one of the least important of these members of my family, you did it for me.'

Matthew 25: 35–40 (Christianity)

Misers do not go to the heavens of the gods… but those who are noble find joy in generosity, and this gives them joy in higher worlds.

Dhammapada 177 (Buddhism)

Better he who shows a smiling face than he who offers milk to drink.

Ketubot 111 (Judaism)

*Do your work with the **welfare** of others always in mind.*

Bhagavad Gita 4 (Hinduism)

Those who believe, and do deeds of righteousness, and establish regular prayers and regular charity, will have their reward with their Lord.

Surah 2: 277 (Islam)

Activity

Further activity

1 Look closely at the pictures and captions. There are five religions represented. Can you tell which they are? Write down the clues you can see, you may need to use the internet to research some of the organizations mentioned.

2 Look at the quotes above. They are all from holy books. Decide which quote you think goes with which picture.

3 Devise a questionnaire to use with the class to investigate how many people in the class have helped someone during the last month. Your results should show why they decided to help and what they did.

Thought diary

During the next week note down in your Thought diary what people *did* to help you in any way.

Key Words

Charity – *Organization which raises money for a particular cause.*

Parable – *Short story which aims to teach you something about how to behave.*

Welfare – *Well-being and health.*

Service to all

**VOLUNTEERS NEEDED
TO HELP INFANT SCHOOL
CHILDREN PLAY FOOTBALL**

PAUL: Miss, on the RE notice-board there's a job advertised helping kids at the infant school to play football. How much do you get paid?

TEACHER: You don't get paid, Paul. Brakenwood Infant School wants some of our pupils to go once a week to coach the football team. They're hoping to enter the championship this year.

PAUL: But why go if you're not going to get paid? That's slave labour! No point going if you're not going to get anything out of it!

Activity

1 Was Paul right? Write down your answer explaining the reason for your decision.

2 Although Paul was not going to be paid, discuss with a partner what Paul might have gained by helping out. Then create a dialogue between the teacher and Paul where she tries to explain to him the importance of taking part.

Sewa

Many people throughout the world take part in some form of **voluntary service**. For Sikhs, **sewa**, or service to others, is a central part of their religion. By giving service to other people, Sikhs believe that they are worshipping God. A Sikh is expected to help through individual and group actions. This may be giving money or food but often involves using skills and giving time to do unpaid jobs for people or to help with the cleaning and maintaining of the **gurdwara**.

It does not matter how wealthy a Sikh is; they would be expected to do tasks such as cleaning the gurdwara floor, serving the food in the **langar** or doing the washing-up after the communal meal. Volunteers take turns to prepare and cook vegetarian meals for anyone to enjoy.

Sewa does not mean just helping Sikhs but all people.

The **Guru Granth Sahib Ji** states that:

A place in God's Court can only be attained if we do service to others in the world.

Guru Granth Sahib Ji 26

A Sikh soldier was once seen on the battlefield taking water to the wounded and dying. As his fellow soldiers watched him they were angry to discover that he was giving water to the enemy as well. When they reported him to the **Guru Gobind Singh Ji** he told them that he was pleased with the water carrier. He even gave him ointment to take to the enemy. He told them that to help anyone in need was to be a true Sikh.

Activity

Further activity

1 Explain how you think offering service to other people may be considered a way of worshipping God.

2 Read the text here again and look at the quotes on page 25. How many reasons can you find to explain why Sikhs take part in sewa? Try to explain them in your own words.

Thought diary

You have seen the way many Sikhs use their skills to help others. What skills do you have that you could offer to help other people? In the last week who has used their skills to help you?

Key Words

Gurdwara – *Sikh place of worship.*

Guru Gobind Singh Ji – *The tenth Sikh guru.*

Guru Granth Sahib Ji – *Sikh scriptures, sometimes called the Adi Granth.*

Guru Nanak Dev Ji – *The first Sikh Guru.*

Langar – *The dining hall at the gurdwara, and the food served in it.*

Sewa – *Service, helping others.*

Voluntary service – *Unpaid actions you do to help others.*

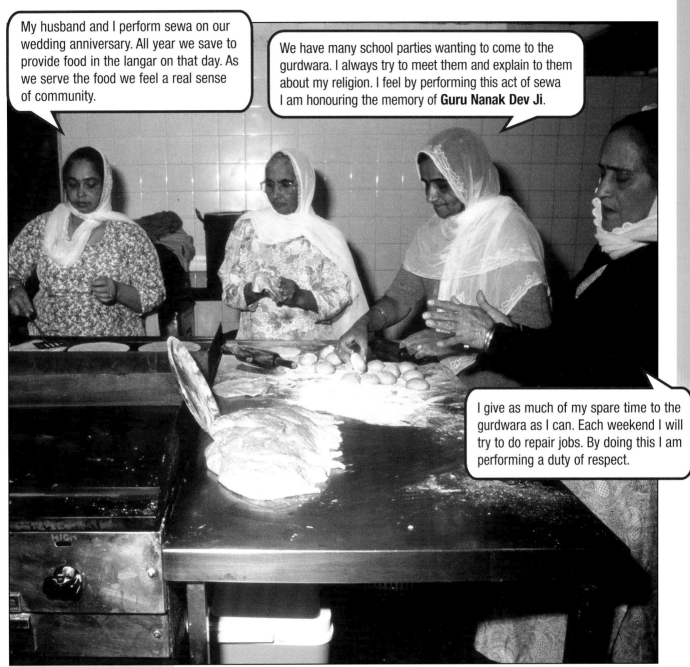

My husband and I perform sewa on our wedding anniversary. All year we save to provide food in the langar on that day. As we serve the food we feel a real sense of community.

We have many school parties wanting to come to the gurdwara. I always try to meet them and explain to them about my religion. I feel by performing this act of sewa I am honouring the memory of **Guru Nanak Dev Ji**.

I give as much of my spare time to the gurdwara as I can. Each weekend I will try to do repair jobs. By doing this I am performing a duty of respect.

Preparing the langar in the Gurdwara

Speaking out

'What makes you angry, Mum?' I asked.

'When people lie and cheat and steal.
But most of all people
Who couldn't care less
How other people feel.'

From *Standing on the Sidelines* by
John Foster

We all have times when we are angry – sometimes because of what is happening around us and to us and sometimes because of what is happening far away to people we read about or see on television.

Activity

1 Draw three large circles in your book.

  a In circle one, write or draw the events that are happening locally that make you angry. You can include events in your own life.

  b In circle two, write or draw the events that are happening in other parts of the world that make you angry.

  c In circle three, write or draw the events that are happening to this planet and to animals that make you angry.

2 Discuss with a partner what you could do to show you are angry and make a difference.

Making a stand

Many of the religious leaders have had to give unpopular messages to people about actions that were happening at that time. This resulted in them showing **righteous anger**. Sometimes this caused trouble with the authorities who consider a religious person should not speak out against events happening in the town.

When the Prophet Muhammad (pbuh) began to preach in **Makkah**, the people did not like his criticism of their lives and the way that they worshipped **idols**. Some people even tried to kill the Prophet.

In Mark 11 in the Bible, we can read how Jesus also became unpopular because he refused to stand by and watch how the Holy Temple in Jerusalem was being used like a market place. Like the Prophet Muhammad (pbuh), Jesus knew it was important to speak out and take action.

The Tabloid Bible interprets certain parts of the Bible as if they were being written for newspapers today. This is their version of the story.

A PAIN IN THE TEMPLE

Jesus clears out money lenders

'Whatever happened to "Blessed are the peacemakers"?' says shocked trader

Following his triumphant entry into the city, Jesus went straight to the Temple and THREW OUT all the tradesmen!

'He was really steamed up', said a stallholder. 'I don't know about Jesus being meek and mild, the way he picked up my stall and threw it through the air was positively superhuman.'

Jesus was reacting to the trading activities that took place in the outer court of the Temple. Here traders sell doves, sheep and cows for sacrifice and change currency to pay the Temple tax.

Jesus's move apparently had popular support.

'People are fed up of being ripped off,' said one visitor. 'Have you seen the price of those doves? Jesus was striking a blow for all of us. I don't see why worship should cost us so much. It was great watching him chuck all their stuff out of the door.'

Christ driving the merchants from the Temple

Activity

Further activity

1 With a partner, look through a newspaper and create a collage of events that are happening in the world today that Jesus might have been angry about.

2 By each example you have found make a reference to Jesus's teachings or actions which would show why he was angry. For example next to a picture of war you could write 'Jesus said "Love your enemies"'.

Key Words

Idols – *Images of gods.*

Makkah – *City where the Prophet Muhammad (pbuh) was born.*

Righteous anger – *Anger or disgust at bad behaviour and events.*

Thought diary

Has there been anything you have read or seen which you knew was wrong but you did nothing about? How did you feel? Why did you decide not to make a stand?

Out of sight, out of mind?

Should we care about what happens thousands of miles away? What is so important that you would leave your home and family for it? Just who are we responsible for?

Activity

Close your eyes for two minutes. Think about what is happening in the world that you think is wrong.

- Open your eyes and make a note of all you had thought of.

- Now make a group of four. Each member of the group should write down their concerns on a piece of paper chain.

- Display your paper chains in the classroom.

James Mawdsley is a Christian **human rights** protester. He cared so much about what was happening in a country thousands of miles away that he risked being arrested and tortured.

James was angry when he learnt how the people of Karen were often **persecuted** by the Burmese army – 30,000 of the Karen people had been killed in the past ten years. As a Christian James looked at the teachings of the Bible for his **inspiration**.

The New Testament reads:

> *If an **authority** is doing things that are against the teaching of Jesus then we must obey God, not men.*
>
> Acts 5: 29

James knew what he had to do.

James Mawdsley with his mother and father

James knew he had to make a stand.
He said:

I cannot sit idle; their cause is my cause.

He went to Rangoon in Burma to start peaceful protests and draw attention to what was happening. One day he had begun to give out stickers to highlight his **campaign** when suddenly he was dragged into a wagon and questioned for four hours. During that time he was blindfolded and tortured. He was then sentenced to five months in a prison cell that measued ten feet by eight feet. After nine weeks, he was given a Bible and while he read it he knew that he was there to serve God. He spent 99 days in that prison cell on his own and then was released back to England.

James could not rest. He knew that he still had to help so he went back and once again started to distribute leaflets. Soon he was dragged away by the police and sentenced to seventeen years in jail. He was given very little food and lived in dreadful conditions. When he complained that he shared his cell with rats, cats, bats and toads, the prison guards took the cats away so that the rats multiplied.

I cannot sit idle; their cause is my cause.

After much pressure from his family, he was eventually released to return to England. James had spent 400 days in a prison cell measuring 27 feet by 23 feet. When James returned to England, he said:

We see the suffering in Burma and claim that it has nothing to do with us. Yet it continues because people believe the problem is not their responsibility.

As a mother I wish he was home, but as a member of the human race I cannot argue with what he is doing.

James' mother

Activity

Further activity

1 Why do you think James wanted to read the Bible when he was in prison?

2 Are problems in other countries our responsibility? Remember to give reasons to back up your answer.

3 Write a short play between James and his mother before he went away and after he came back. In your script try to include the words responsibility, bystander, inspiration and service.

Thought diary

As a member of the human race what would you want to make a protest about? Try to think of a local, national and global example.

Key Words

Authority – *People, like the police, who have a lot of power.*

Campaign – *An organized operation with a purpose.*

Human rights – *Basic rights of all for fair treatment.*

Inspiration – *Something that gives you new ideas and enthusiasm.*

Persecuted – *Ill treatment of people, harassment.*

Assessment

We will go before God to be judged and God will ask us, 'Where are your wounds?' And we will say, 'We have no wounds.' And God will ask, 'Was nothing worth fighting for?'

Rev. Allan Boesak, a leading figure in South Africa's struggle against apartheid

In this chapter you have begun to think about the responsibility you have to other people. You have probably begun to realise the different ways you can show you care.

Here are a few questions that you might have thought about in each unit:

1 *Standing by – What tells us the difference between right and wrong?*

2 *Bystanding – How would we react if our friends were being threatened?*

3 *Actions speak louder than words – Why do many religious believers think it is important to help other people?*

4 *Service to all – What can be gained from taking part in voluntary service?*

5 *Speaking out – What would make Jesus angry today?*

6 *Out of sight, out of mind?– Why should we help people we do not know?*

Reflecting on your progress

1 To help you reflect on what you have learnt from this chapter, look back on your work, or in your Thought diary, and write a few lines on each of the following areas, giving reasons to improve your answers:

   (a) What I enjoyed. Why?

   (b) What I found difficult. Why?

2 Pick an idea that you had and try to explain it clearly to another person. Think about:

- Where the idea came from.
- What the idea is about.
- Why you like the idea.
- The *best* way to explain it to someone.

3 In your Thought diary, copy down five **skills** that you have used most during this chapter from the following list:

- I listened well to others.
- I gave reasons for my views.
- I expressed myself clearly.
- I tried to imagine other people's points of view.
- I developed my writing and artistic skills.
- I investigated a new topic by myself.
- I kept on task well.
- I used lots of imagination.
- I cared about the feelings of other people.
- I gave justified views.

4 What facts did you learn? What do you understand now that you did not know about before? Make a spider diagram or a poster to show your thoughts.

Test yourself

❶ *Give an example of an individual who has refused to be a bystander. Explain why they decided to get involved and the action they took. [Level 4 – AT2]*

❷ *Re read the definition of conscience on page 19. Imagine you had to explain it to a person without using words. Devise a logo, symbol or sequence of pictures which you think conveys the meaning. [Level 4 – AT2]*

❸ *You have considered many different reasons why people decided not to be bystanders to events that they knew were wrong. Why do you think it is important to take action? [Level 5 – AT2]*

❹ *Imagine someone said to you 'Religious people should stick to worshipping God not trying to help others'. After reading this chapter how would you respond? Give reasons for your answer and refer to more than one religious teaching. [Level 6 – AT2]*

Where next?

❶ *Look at the list of skills opposite. Choose two that you want to improve on in the future. Perhaps you could note them down in your Thought diary. (Describe two ways in which you could improve them. Is there someone who could give you suggestions? Is there some way of reminding yourself of your aims in future lessons?)*

❷ *Think about the topic you enjoyed most. What could you do to investigate it further? Are there any websites or books that could help you find out more?*

Well done!

You know more, have thought more and improved your skills. KEEP GOING! ✔

The meaning of power

In this chapter you will consider what power is and how it can be used to good and bad effect by focusing on Judaism, Christianity, Islam and Sikhism.

Power is defined in the Illustrated Oxford English dictionary as:

> *The ability to do or act.*
>
> *A government, influence or authority.*
>
> *An influential person, group or organization.*

When we think about the word 'power', certain images come to mind. We imagine strength, courage and muscles. Do you think people today want to be powerful? Do we see having power as something that will lead to increased respect?

We see power every day. Parents wield power over children, teachers over students, policemen over the public and politicians over society. In films and on TV we see superheroes using their power to save the world against evil. Their power is often superhuman – something that is far superior to the power of mere humans.

Here are some examples of superheroes. Are there any clues to show that they are indeed powerful?

They all have certain powers.

Spiderman

Superman

Activity

1 If you could have a super human power, what power would you have and why?

2 How would you use your power? Would you use it for good or evil? Explain your answer.

3 When we talk about power, we can mean being physically strong. Are men physically stronger than women? What do you think? Do women have power that men do not have?

Activity

Further activity

1 Who is the most powerful person you know? What is it they do that makes them powerful?

2 The Prime Minister is seen as a powerful person, someone who can use his power to make a difference. If you had the power to make a difference, what would you do and why?

3 Think about the people you admire. Why do you admire them? Are these people who have power? What kind of power do they have?

Pop stars, film stars and sports stars all have power – the power to stir passion and emotion within us. No doubt you have all watched films and felt a tug on your heart strings or shed a tear. Songs can remind us of particular moments in our lives and cause us to feel particular emotions – sometimes it is love, sometimes hurt and pain, and sometimes it reminds us of a time when we were very happy.

Do you think pop stars have the same kind of power that politicians do? Discuss with a partner the differences between them and which you think is more important.

Lots of pop stars sing about the power of love. Imagine you are designing a CD cover for a single that is all about 'The Power of Love'. How will you communicate this to people? (Remember love can cause people to be sad as well as happy!)

People cry for lots of different reasons. Is crying a sign of strength or weakness? Explain your thoughts.

Think of a time when you cried in front of others. Did you try to stop yourself from crying? Why?

Power

Power is an amazing thing – it cannot be seen by the naked eye, but it does have an incredible effect on people. Some people face very difficult life changing situations, but they do not give up. Instead they use their power to achieve great things. Lance Armstrong was one of the best cyclists in the world when he was diagnosed with having cancer in 1996. He was given only a 50 per cent chance of surviving but he endured painful treatment to overcome the disease. He was able to take up cycling again and went on to win the 1999 Tour de France. Despite having a terrible illness he did not give up and has since used his power positively to raise awareness and funds to help others who are dealing with cancer.

Reflection

Do you know of anyone else who has used their own power to overcome difficulties? Or someone who has been affected by a tragedy who has then moved on to help others in need?

Try to find out about someone who has used their power to do this.

Thought diary

You have been thinking about power in this unit. Create a spider diagram using all the words you would use when thinking about power.

Key Words

Power – *Capability to do something, a great force or might, an influential person or group.*

Positive and negative power

Have you ever been in a position of power? It may be that you have been captain of a football team, a leader in a group or you may be an older brother or sister. Having power can be fantastic: you are in charge, have responsibility and you can tell people what to do! Lots of people use their power wisely, helping others.

But power can also lead to people becoming power crazy. Some people abuse their power and become corrupt, using their power to further their own ends so that they can become richer or even more powerful. These people often think about themselves rather than others.

In China during the 1940s, people were incredibly poor. Mao Tse Tung, a rebel leader, and his band of followers created an air of hope for those who had no hope. He and his army fought the Chinese Government's Red Army and eventually, after many battles, defeated them. Mao was able to claim victory.

Mao Tse Tung

When Mao Tse Tung took over the Government, people believed he was their **saviour**, their hero. This man was going to provide the answer to all their problems. The people believed that he would bring an end to poverty and hunger.

Unfortunately, these hopes and dreams of a better life were short lived. The power went to Mao's head and, along with his wife, he created a country where suspicion and fear were present each day. People were scared to speak their minds, for if they said anything that was in opposition to the Government of China, they could be arrested and imprisoned.

Chairman Mao spoke and the people listened. They believed his were the words of the wise. Anhua Gao in her book *To the Edge of the Sky* describes how leaflets were distributed on her school campus reporting how Chairman Mao said:

*We must destroy the **reactionary** old-age tradition of respecting the teachers.*

His words led to teachers being abused by their students. Chairman Mao was indeed a powerful man. His words caused the people of China to act cruelly toward their fellow human beings.

This example of someone who used their power badly is quite extreme, but there are people all over the world who use their power in similar ways.

Activity

Can you think of anyone who has used their power in a way you think is questionable? It may be a politician, a teacher or a parent. It may be someone in the UK or elsewhere in the world. Share your thoughts with a partner.

An example of someone who used their power to save others is remembered during the Jewish festival of **Hannukah**.

At this time women are remembered for the role they played in helping the Jews to stand firm against the Syrians. The Syrians were trying to overpower the Jewish people and force them to worship idols rather than God.

One woman who was seen as very brave was called Judith. She crept into a Syrian army camp. The Syrian General Holofernes saw Judith and fell in love with her. He invited her to make a meal for him. Judith carefully prepared his meal using lots of cheese to make him thirsty. The General drank lots of wine and eventually fell asleep. Judith seized her opportunity and cut off his head!

She took the head back to the Jews, who immediately felt brave enough to stand up to the Syrian army. A battle was fought and the Jewish people were victorious.

Activity

1 What power did Judith have and how did she use it?

2 Imagine you are writing a newspaper article about Judith and what she did. What would your headline be? What would your article say? Do you think she did the right thing? Is it acceptable to respond to a situation using violence? Illustrate your story with a picture.

Activity

Further activity

Some religions use their power to tell people how they should behave, giving them rules to follow. In the Old Testament in the Bible, there are the Ten Commandments. These rules are part of Judaism and Christianity and are written here.

1 You shall have no other gods before me.

2 Do not worship false idols.

3 You shall not **blaspheme**.

4 Keep the Sabbath holy.

5 Honour your parents.

6 You shall not kill.

7 You shall not commit adultery.

8 You shall not steal.

9 You shall not lie.

10 Do not desire what is not yours.

Do you think these rules show religion using its power wisely? Explain your thinking.

If you were in a position of power, what would be your eleventh commandment?

Thought diary

You have seen some examples of where power has been misused, which has led to some horrible events happening. Do people who have power have a certain responsibility to use it wisely? Why?

Key Words

Blaspheme – *To use religious terms without respect.*

Hannukah – *An eight day festival of lights to celebrate the re-dedication of the temple after victory over the Greeks.*

Reactionary – *A conservative approach to something, someone opposed to progress.*

Saviour – *A person who rescues or saves others.*

The power of authority

Have you ever had to stand up to someone? It may be that a friend has said something you disagree with and has expected you to agree with them, or that they have tried to persuade you to do something you do not really want to do, such as skip lessons or a whole day at school! To stand up to someone takes courage and is not always easy to do.

When faced with pressure it is very difficult to stay true to your beliefs. People who are the victims of bullies often find it hard to stand up to the bully alone. They need the help and support of others. Recently we have seen several cases where pupils in schools have been bullied so badly that they have left school. One girl has even written to Tony Blair to ask him to appoint a Children's Commissioner, so that children with problems have someone they can talk to who will help them through.

Nelson Mandela

Nelson Mandela was born in South Africa in 1918 a time when black people were treated as second-class citizens. The ruling class were white and had the power to tell black people where they should live, what jobs they could do, where they could work, what time they had to be in at night and what meetings they could hold. The black people had no rights; they were not even allowed to vote. The system of government was called **apartheid**.

Activity

1 Do you think apartheid is an acceptable way for a government to run a country? Give reasons for your answers.

2 If you lived in a country where you were being treated as a second-class citizen, would you take action? Why? How? What difficulties might you face in trying to stand up to the system?

Nelson Mandela believed that the government of his country was completely unfair. He believed that everyone should have a say in how the country was run. So he held meetings to achieve this goal. He did not believe in using violence. He was arrested on many occasions and he knew that he could be sent to prison at any time. This would mean he would not be able to see his wife and children. However, Mandela was convinced he had to keep going.

For many years Mandela was hunted by the police and spent time in prison. In 1962 he was arrested and sentenced to five years in prison. Whilst serving this sentence he was charged with **conspiracy** to commit **treason** and sentenced to life imprisonment. People throughout the world continued his work, fighting for the equal treatment of all people in South Africa and for his release from prison. After serving 28 years in prison he was released.

He wrote in his book, *The Long Walk to Freedom*:

*A man who takes away another man's freedom is a prisoner of hatred, he is locked behind the bars of **prejudice** and narrow-mindedness… to be free is… to live in a way that respects and enhances the freedom of others… with freedom comes responsibilities.*

Activity

As a class, discuss what Nelson Mandela meant. Then, in pairs, produce a collage/poster/artwork to represent his words.

Mandela never gave up: despite everything that was happening and the risks he took, he stayed true to his beliefs. Other people do not have this strength.

In the Bible we are told that after Jesus was arrested and while he was being questioned by the High Priest, Peter, one of his disciples, waited outside to see what was going to happen to him.

While he was waiting, several people approached him and asked him if he was a friend of Jesus. Each time this happened, Peter denied knowing him. He was frightened that if he admitted to being a friend of Jesus he would be arrested too.

He denied knowing Jesus three times during the night. After his third denial, the cock crowed three times and Peter remembered something Jesus had said.

Jesus said to Peter, 'I tell you that before the cock crows tonight, you will say three times that you do not know me.'

Peter answered, 'I will never say that, even if I have to die with you!'

Matthew 26: 34–35

Peter felt ashamed that he had let Jesus down. He had not stood up to be counted as a follower of Jesus.

Activity

Further activity

1 Peter denied knowing Jesus. Does this mean he was a weak person? Explain your answer.

2 Nelson Mandela stood up for what he believed, even though he knew he was risking his freedom. What qualities did he need to do this?

3 Imagine for a moment that you are passionate about learning. You believe that everyone has a right to an education, but the Government has decided that education is only for pupils with blond hair. Would you protest against this new law, even though it might mean you go to prison? Explain why.

Thought diary

People today protest regularly about all sorts of things. They stand up for the things they believe in. Thinking about some of the issues raised in this unit, produce a poster or a leaflet about some of the things you think are important in life.

If any of these things were threatened, would you take action to protect them? Why? What form would your action take?

Key Words

Apartheid – *An Afrikaner word meaning 'separation'. It was a system of government used in South Africa from 1948 to the early 1990s where white people were seen as being better than black people and they were kept apart by law.*

Conspiracy – *Secret plan for a group to act together.*

Prejudice – *An opinion formed without knowledge or reason.*

Treason – *Planning to overthrow the government.*

The power of God

God is believed to be all-knowing (**omniscient**) and all-powerful (**omnipotent**). He is a being that can do whatever he wants. His power knows no ends. God knows everything, sees everything and can act in any way he chooses.

Some people believe that God is constantly acting in the world. Can you think of any things that happen today that some people might see as being the work of God? Is the sun rising each day the work of God? Is someone recovering from an illness an act of God? Can we always see his actions?

Activity

Can you think of any examples people might give of God acting in the world today? Share your thoughts with a partner.

A Jewish perspective

Religious believers consider God to have power over everything and they believe he has used this power to cause things in the past. These events are remembered today in festivals and celebrations. One such event is remembered in Judaism when God used his power to **liberate** the Israelites from slavery. This famous story took place a long time ago in Egypt and is told in the book of **Exodus** in the Bible.

The **Pharaoh** had taken the Israelites as his slaves. They were being treated cruelly and Moses was chosen by God as the man to lead the Israelites out of Egypt and to a new homeland. God told Moses to go and see the Pharaoh and ask him to set the Israelites free. Unfortunately the Pharaoh did not listen. This was when the ten plagues began.

The Egyptians woke up and wanted to bathe in the river, but to their horror the water had turned to blood! More plagues were sent but still the Pharaoh would not let the Israelites go!

Moses returned to see the Pharaoh again and asked him to release the Israelites.

'What? You expect me to set you slaves free? What will become of our building programme? Who will dig, make bricks and create a country that will be the envy of the world over? You expect me, the Pharaoh of Egypt, to be scared of God? Does he not realize I am the Pharaoh?'

Moses responded by reminding the Pharaoh of the destruction and havoc already caused by God.

'Do you really want to put your people through more trouble, make their lives even more unbearable? Listen to me – my God can do whatever he wants and there is nothing He will not do to set His people free.'

The Pharaoh did not listen. Slavery continued and God sent even more plagues to strike against the Egyptians. Finally the tenth plague arrived – the angel of death. God warned Moses to tell all the Israelites to pack their belongings and be ready to leave. That night they were to kill a lamb and put some of its blood on the doorpost. The Israelites were a little puzzled but did as they were told.

God told His angel to visit the house of anyone who did not have blood on the doorpost and to kill the first-born child.

The next day the Egyptian families woke up and found to their horror that their eldest children had been killed. The Pharaoh was devastated and ordered the Israelites to leave at once. This they did, but they had no time to wait for their bread to rise, so they took flat bread with them.

The Pharaoh sent his army after the slaves but the Israelites had made it to the edge of the Red Sea. Moses prayed to God, and the Israelites watched in amazement as the sea parted to the right and to the left allowing them to walk through to safety. The Israelites made it through, but the Egyptian army followed and were swallowed up in the sea!

The power of God had saved the Israelites. Today, Jews remember this event in the festival of the Passover, a celebration of freedom.

Passover (**Pesach**) is celebrated in the spring and lasts for eight days. During this time Jews do not eat any food that has any yeast in it. Can you think why?

The foods eaten during the special Passover meal are symbolic – they represent an event in the story of the Exodus, the Israelites being set free from Egypt.

Some of the foods used in the meal are listed here:

- a lamb bone
- unleavened bread made without yeast (matzah)
- bitter herbs
- haroset – a mixture of chopped apples, nuts and wine
- a green vegetable
- an egg.

Can you think of anything these foods may represent?

Activity

1 What does the story of the ten plagues tell you about God's power?

2 Imagine the plagues were to happen today. How would people react? Would they see it as evidence of God's power? Explain your views.

3 With a partner, role-play the discussion that takes place between the Pharaoh and Moses. How could Moses persuade the Pharaoh to let the people go? How might the Pharaoh respond?

Thought diary

Should God always be the one responsible for solving problems in the world? Explain your thoughts.

Key Words

Exodus – *A large group of people leaving somewhere.*
Liberate – *To set free.*
Omnipotent – *All-powerful.*
Omniscient – *All-knowing.*
Pesach – *The Hebrew word for Passover.*
Pharaoh – *The leader of Egypt.*

The power of me!

When we think of power, we often forget that we all have power ourselves. We have the power to achieve more than we realize.

Activity

1 Thomas Edison, the inventor of light bulbs, said:

> *If we all did the things we are truly capable of doing, we would literally **astound** ourselves.*

What do you think he meant by this? Is he implying that we are lazy and settle for second best?

2 Think about your life in the future. What things would you like to have achieved by the time you are 30? Draw a picture to show what you hope your life will be like when you are 30 years old.

3 How are you going to achieve these things? Make a list of the things you need to do now to make sure that you get there.

Some people believe that to be successful you have to show self-discipline and self-control. This means that you resist **temptation** and do the right thing. Think about your own life. No doubt at some point you have been faced with a choice – seeing friends, watching TV, anything but settling down to tackle your homework.

If you choose to tackle your homework and complete it all before the date it is due to be handed in, then you have resisted temptation and shown self-discipline and self-control.

If you choose to stay out with your friends and not do your homework, facing your teacher with the excuse that the dog ate it, unfortunately you have given in to temptation and shown no self-discipline or self-control.

The Islamic view

Muslims believe that life is a struggle in which we are constantly fighting temptations. Temptations can be telling lies to our parents, thinking bad thoughts about our friends, or hurting someone. To overcome temptation is a struggle. This fight is known as the **greater jihad**, the struggle against evil in yourself. The lesser jihad is the fight against evil within your community.

Activity

1 Jot down some thoughts about things that people your age can be tempted to do.

2 Why do you think some people give in to temptation and other people do not?

3 Is it easy to resist temptation? Explain your answer.

4 Why do you think Muslims call the fight against evil within yourself the 'greater jihad' and the fight against evil within the community the 'lesser jihad'?

Each year there is a 24-hour famine in aid of charity. People in the UK do not eat for 24 hours raising money to help people in the developing world who do not have enough food. Would you stop eating for 24 hours? How easy would this be? What would be the hardest food to give up?

Muslims fast each year for a month. This is known as **sawm** and it is the fourth pillar of Islam, one of their key beliefs. They fast during the month of Ramadan. During this month no food or drink must pass the lips during daylight hours. They also try to give up bad thoughts and bad behaviour. Again, this pillar shows the ability to resist temptation and demonstrate self-discipline. It also helps Muslims to understand what it is like to be poor and hungry.

Christians also have a time of year when they give something up. This period of time is known as **Lent** and lasts for 40 days just before Easter. During this time many Christians will 'give up something for Lent.' Some people choose to give up chocolate or crisps, other people try to give up something that could be a little more difficult such as swearing, and for 40 days they do not eat chocolate or crisps or they do not swear.

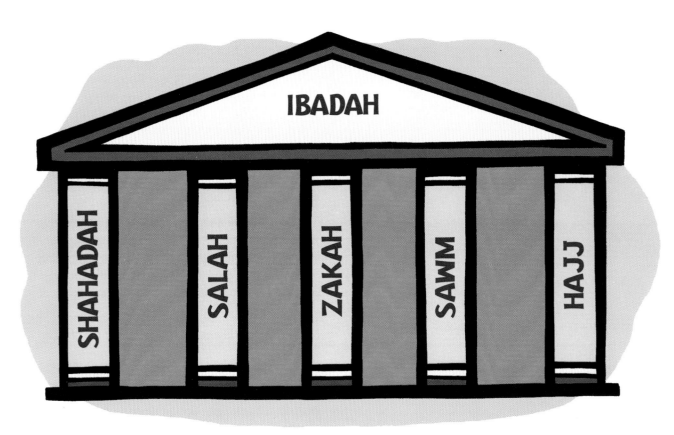

Reflection

Why do you think giving up swearing could be harder to do that giving up chocolate or crisps?

At this time Christians remember when Jesus spent 40 days in the desert being tempted by the Devil. The Devil tried to get Jesus to bow down and worship him, but Jesus refused and stayed true to God.

Activity

Further activity

1 Muslims believe you have the power to resist temptation. However, some temptations are easier to resist than others. What do you think would be the hardest thing to give up – food, thoughts or deeds? Why?

2 Do you think people in rich countries use their power over themselves at all? If so, how and why?

3 Do people in rich countries appreciate things like food or do they take it for granted? Can you think of anything else people take for granted? Share your thoughts with a partner.

Thought diary

You have been thinking about temptation and having the strength of character to resist temptation. Would you rob a bank if you knew you would get away with £1,000 and not get caught?

Jot down your reasons for your actions.

Key Words

Astound – *To overcome with amazement.*

Greater jihad – *A Muslim belief meaning to strive against evil within yourself, trying to resist temptation.*

Lent – *Christian festival before Easter remembering when Jesus was tempted by the Devil.*

Sawm – *The fourth pillar of Islam, where Muslims fast during the month of Ramadan.*

Temptation – *To want to do something despite your better judgement.*

Power and belief

Adverts constantly try to persuade us to try new things. The power of suggestion can make us believe that using particular creams, driving a particular car, or wearing particular jeans, will make us look younger, be more attractive or have a fabulous day! You may not believe you are being influenced, but you cannot escape the power of advertising.

Activity

1 Choose an advert that you particularly like. Why do you like it? Would it persuade you to buy the product? Discuss your thoughts with a partner.

2 Can advertising be dangerous? In what ways?

3 Can you think of any adverts that are about helping others or safety.

Of course, with advertising the use of power is controlled. There are people whose job it is to make sure that all adverts tell the truth. Advertisers are not allowed to use their power to make claims that are untrue. But there have been times when people have used their power to cause harm and destruction.

Some people today have tremendous power – just look at the power of politicians. At election time they persuade the public to vote for them, making promises about what they will do if they should get into power. Of course, these promises may not always be fulfilled!

If people want to be in positions of power, should they tell the truth about how they will use their power?

Baisakhi

Sikhs celebrate **Baisakhi** at the start of the Sikh new year, usually on 13 and 14 April. This festival remembers when **Guru Gobind Singh Ji**, one of the ten **Gurus** or teachers in Sikhism, founded the **Khalsa**, the brotherhood of Sikhism.

At the Sikh festival of Baisakhi, Guru Gobind Singh Ji asked if anyone was prepared to lay down their life for God and the Guru. People were shocked and feared they would be killed. But one brave man stepped forward and was taken into a tent. The crowd heard the sound of a sword slicing through the air and then a dull thud as something fell on the floor.

The Guru returned to the audience with a sword dripping with blood. He asked again if anyone would lay down their life. Another man stepped forward and the same thing happened. The Guru took him into the tent, there was the sound of the sword slicing the air and then a dull thud.

The crowd gasped, surely this would not happen again – surely no one else would be killed. But it did, three more times!

The crowd was horrified and feared for their lives. But the five men stepped out of the tent – alive! All were wearing turbans. Guru Gobind Singh Ji shouted to the crowd: 'These men are specially brave, they had faith in me. I want Sikhs to be brave like these men.'

He then went on to tell people that Sikhs should wear turbans and not cut their hair, but wear it fastened in place with a special comb, wear a steel bangle to show strength and courage and carry a sword to protect those in need. This marked the start of the Sikh Khalsa and today Sikhs show their faith by wearing what are known as the Five Ks.

Guru Gobind Singh Ji, like other religious leaders, had the power to convince people to follow him.

Activity

1 Can you think of any reasons why people choose to follow a religious leader and their teachings? Share your ideas with a partner.

2
> *I am more afraid of an army of 100 sheep led by a lion than an army of 100 lions led by one sheep.*
>
> Talleyrand

What does this quote mean?

3 Can you think of any examples where people have used their power to make a positive difference to people's lives?

4 Can you think of any examples where people have used their power to hurt people or cause death?

5 Sometimes people make reference to 'blind faith'. What does this phrase mean? Could it be dangerous to have 'blind faith'?

Activity

Further activity

Choose a person you particularly admire; someone whose views and ideas you listen to. Explain why you admire this person – would you do anything they suggested?

Thought diary

> *My definition of a leader… is a man who can persuade people to do what they don't want to do, or do what they're too lazy to do, and like it.*
>
> Harry S. Truman (1884–1972)

Read the above quote. Thinking about this and your own views on leadership, jot down some thoughts about what being a leader is all about.

Key Words

Baisakhi – *A major Sikh festival celebrating the formation of the Khalsa, 1699.*

Guru – *Teacher in Sikhism.*

Guru Gobind Singh Ji – *The tenth Sikh Guru.*

Khalsa – *Brotherhood of Sikhism.*

Assessment

In this chapter we have been thinking about different aspects of power, what power is, and how it is used. You have probably realized that power is not always such a good thing, depending on the reasons for the behaviour of the individual.

Here are a few questions that you might have thought about in each unit:

❶ *The meaning of power – What do we mean when we talk about power?*

❷ *Positive and negative power – Is power always a good thing?*

❸ *The power of authority – Do we stand up for our beliefs or do we give in?*

❹ *The power of God – What powers of God can be seen in today's world?*

❺ *The power of me – What kinds of power do you have?*

❻ *Power and belief – Are beliefs more powerful than actions?*

Reflecting on your progress

❶ To help you reflect on what you have learnt from this chapter, look back on your work, or in your Thought diary, and write a few lines on each of the following areas, giving reasons to improve your answers:

ⓐ What I enjoyed. Why?

ⓑ What I found difficult. Why?

❷ Pick an idea that you had and try to explain it clearly to another person. Think about:

- Where the idea came from.
- What the idea is about.
- Why you like the idea.
- The *best* way to explain it to someone.

❸ In your Thought diary, copy down five **skills** that you have used during this chapter from the following list:

- I listened well to others.
- I gave reasons for my views.
- I expressed myself clearly.
- I tried to imagine other people's points of view.
- I developed my writing and artistic skills.
- I investigated a new topic by myself.
- I kept on task well.
- I used lots of imagination.
- I cared about the feelings of other people.
- I gave justified views.

❹ What facts did you learn? What do you understand now that you did not know about before? Make a spider diagram or a poster to show your thoughts.

Test yourself

❶ *What does this symbol of power say to you? Explain your answer. [Level 4 – AT2]*

❷ *How have people used their power? Give at least two examples of people who have had power and explain whether they have used it positively or negatively. [Level 5 – AT2]*

❸ *Give an example of how you can show power in your life and how this might affect you or other people around you. This might be in a very small way and only involve you, or it might be a more obvious show of power. Explain your response. [Level 6 – AT2]*

❹

> *I long to accomplish a great and noble task, but it is my chief duty to accomplish humble tasks as though they were great and noble. The world is moved along, not only by the mighty shoves of its heroes, but also by the aggregate of the tiny pushes of each honest worker.*

Helen Keller

ⓐ What do you think Helen Keller means when she refers to a 'humble' task?

ⓑ What do you think she means when she refers to a 'great and noble' task?

ⓒ What do you think the whole quote means? Do you agree with Helen Keller's point of view?

[Level 7 – AT2]

❺ *Who do you think has the most power over you? Explain your answer, giving reasons to support your views. [Level 6 – AT2]*

What next?

❶ *Look at the list of skills opposite. Choose two that you want to improve on in the future. Perhaps you could note them down in your Thought diary. (Describe two ways in which you could improve them. Is there someone who could give you suggestions? Is there some way of reminding yourself of your aims in future lessons?)*

❷ *Think about the topic you enjoyed most. What could you do to investigate it further? Are there any websites or books that could help you find out more?*

Well done!

You know more, have thought more and improved your skills. KEEP GOING! ✓

Space to be me

In this unit you will reflect on your own identity and think about how some people express their beliefs through the clothes they wear, you will recognize that many people need time and space to consider the important things in their lives by looking at Islam, Christianity, Judaism and Hinduism.

Every second of every day, five people are born. That means each day there will be 432,000 babies born. How many people will that be by the end of the lesson? How many by the time that you leave school today?

What is amazing is that every person is an **individual**. They will all lead different lives and have different talents and interests. They will even have different fingerprints! It does not matter how many people are born, each is an individual with their own **identity**. They are a one-off.

Only one of me and nobody can get a second one from a photocopy machine.

James Berry (b. 1924), Jamaican poet

Activity

Think about what makes you special. How are you different to your family? Your friends? All the people you know? Now you are going to create your own identity passport. This is a passport about the real you.

You should include:

- your favourite foods
- what you like to wear
- what you consider is important in your life
- where you like to go
- a symbol on the front which shows the real you.

You should finish your passport by completing the following sentences:

I AM SPECIAL. I AM THE ONLY PERSON I KNOW WHO…

As we get older there are many things about us that will change. Sometimes these will be as a result of the different **influences** on our lives.

Activity

Further activity

1 Look at the picture below. Which do you think has the most influence in your life at the moment? Try to put them in order.

2 Think back to when you were at junior school – what had most influence then? How has your list changed?

3 Why do you think there are different influences at different times of our lives?

4 Design a poster to show what is special and individual about you.

Thought diary

Are there ever times when it is difficult to show the real you? Can you remember a time when you said or did something to be like other people? Try to remember why you did not want to show your individuality.

Key Words

Identity – *The things that make someone who they are.*
Individual – *One particular person rather than a whole group.*
Influences – *The effect someone or something has on you.*

Space to show the real me

Our choice of clothes can say a lot about us. Think about your school uniform. Do you dislike wearing the same clothes as others? Or do you enjoy waking up in the morning not having to think about what to wear? Often the clothes we wear express what we are like as a person. In this unit you will be thinking about how the clothes we wear can give an opportunity to show something about the real you.

Activity

1 Our choice of clothes give lots of clues about the jobs we do, the music we like, or even what we consider to be important. Now it is your chance to be a detective. Look at the pictures above and for each write down anything you can guess about that person from the clothes they wear.

2 Do you have anything you wear which shows something about the real you? It may be a T-shirt which shows where you have been, a football scarf which shows a team you support, or an item of religious clothing or jewellery which shows your beliefs. Perhaps there are other things that go beyond clothing and image? Are there certain places where you feel comfortable wearing that item of clothing? Try to explain why.

Louise and Safia are both thirteen. They have been best friends since primary school.

LOUISE: Safia, is everything okay? Why were you and your mum coming out of the head teacher's office?

SAFIA: Everything's fine. I didn't want to tell you until it was for certain, but I'm going to be wearing the **hijab** in school from the start of next term.

LOUISE: What! They're making you cover your hair? Who's forcing you to do that? Is it your mum or the **imam** at the mosque?

SAFIA: You've got it so wrong. No one is forcing me – I want to do it. I've wanted to for ages but Mum has kept telling me to wait until I'm really sure of what it means to wear it. It's a real **commitment**. Not just something you wear on days you feel like it. By wearing it I'm showing something about me.

LOUISE: Like what?

SAFIA: Well, firstly, I feel a sense of identity with my religion, Islam – I am obeying what it says in the **Qur'an** and showing what I believe to be true. A sense of pride in my own identity.

LOUISE: But what will the others say in the class? What happens if they laugh at you?

SAFIA: That's up to them really, isn't it? When I had finally made my decision, Mum and I thought it was important to go to the head teacher and explain. I think she was quite impressed by the way I had really considered everything. As to the others in the class – if they are true friends then I am sure they will understand the importance of giving me the space to show the real me.

Activity

Further activity

1 Explain in your own words why you think Safia has decided to wear the hijab.

2 With your partner, act out the conversation which might have taken place in the head teacher's office. Remember, Safia would give justified views as to why she wanted to wear the hijab.

Thought diary

How could your school give you space to show the real you? Jot down your ideas. How might other people in the school be affected?

Key Words

Commitment – *Promise.*

Hijab – *Head-covering worn by some Muslim women.*

Imam – *A person who leads the communal prayer for Muslims.*

Qur'an – *Holy book of Islam.*

Space to find me

What is important in your life? Who gives you hope for the future? What are you going to do with your life?

No time to think about it? No place to think about it? From the time you get up in the morning until the time you go to bed is there ever a time and place when you can sit and think about these big questions about the real you?

The singer John Denver wrote many of his songs when he was in the countryside away from traffic and noise.

And I look into space
Tryin' find out who I am
And I'm looking to know and understand.
All alone in the universe,
sometimes that's how it seems.
I get lost in the madness and screams.

From *Looking For Space* by John Denver

Activity

1 With a partner, write down a list of all the distractions and noises you hear each day. Highlight those that did not exist 50 years ago, for example, mobile phones.

2 Do you have a place you can go to find peace, somewhere that is not 'lost in the madness and screams'? It may be somewhere in your house or somewhere you have visited when you have been on holiday. Close your eyes and try to remember why you find peace there. Is it quiet? Are you with people you trust? What are the colours you remember? Where do you sit or lie? Is there any noise?

3 Now draw a picture of that place and, through your drawing, try to show what makes that place a special space for you.

Times of relection on a retreat

During the last ten years it has become popular for people, religious or not, to spend a few days at a **retreat** centre. Sometimes the centre is run by a particular religion but some centres are for anyone who wants to get away from distractions in life and to think about really important issues.

A retreat offers the opportunity to think about what is really important in your life and to find peace within yourself. Many retreat centres do not allow televisions or mobile phones so that people will not be **distracted**. Indeed, in some retreat centres people are only allowed to talk at certain times of the day.

Sometimes people might go on a retreat before making a big decision in their life. Roman Catholic teenagers often go on retreat before they take the step of being **confirmed**.

Martin is in Year 8 at school. He is a Roman Catholic and about to be confirmed. This means he has chosen to confirm the promises his godparents made for him when he was a baby. From now on he will be seen as an adult in the Catholic Church. To prepare for this he has been attending weekly classes for about six months to learn more about his religion. As part of his preparation for confirmation he and his confirmation class are attending a three-day retreat.

Dear Diary,

Well, it's not like I imagined. I thought it was going to be really boring without the TV but I haven't missed it at all. This morning when I got up the only noise I could hear was the birds singing. There was no radio playing, no little brother screaming, no Mum telling me I was late for school and no doors slamming. Just birds singing. After attending morning **mass** we had breakfast and then were told we could go out into the grounds and think about the responsibility we were about to take on now we are going to be confirmed. As I walked out I just felt so calm and peaceful.

I actually did sit under a tree and think about the reading I heard at breakfast. We were told about a man called Sean Devereux who campaigned against young boys becoming child soldiers in Liberia and Somalia. Boys who are only my age. Although he was threatened, he still spoke out. Then he was shot by an unknown person. It really made me think of how he had died for what he believed in. I'd never really thought before about the strength people's faith can give them to do what they know to be right. I've been attending these classes, but I had never really stopped to think just what it was I was doing. Now here I am about to make a commitment with my life.

It's scary really, because I began to think about what I really wanted to do with my life and what was really important.

Thought diary

In the past year, what new responsibilities have you taken on? You might have started to bring a younger brother to school or looked after a pet on your own. Highlight any new responsibilities that you have had to prepare for in some way.

Activity

Further activity

1 Why do you think many people who are preparing for confirmation choose to go on a retreat?

2 Sean Devereux once wrote, 'When my heart beats I have to do what I think I can do, that is, to help those who are less fortunate than ourselves.'

Draw a circle in the middle of a piece of paper. In the circle write 'What I think I can do'. Now from the circle create a spider diagram of all those things that you think you could do with your life.

Key Words

Confirmed – *One of the seven sacraments in the Roman Catholic Church.*

Distracted – *Attention diverted from work or thoughts.*

Mass – *Service celebrating the death and resurrection of Jesus using bread and wine.*

Retreat – *A place where people can attend without distractions.*

51

Space to show what I believe

you're not old enough yet!

Why don't you grow up?

Act your age!

Heard it all before?

But when do we start to make adult decisions? What happens if those decisions are different from those of our family and friends? We are not **clones** of each other. As we grow older we will start to do and believe in things differently to our family and friends.

The Day I Became a Vegetarian

When I was seven and a half,
I decided to become a vegetarian.

When I arrived home from school,
I told my Mum.
'That's fine,' she said.
'It's up to you what you eat.
We're having meat.
The vegetables are over there.'

An hour later
When Dad came home,
I sat down to eat
Like the rest of the family.
I'd decided to give up
Being a vegetarian.

From *Standing on the Sidelines* by John Foster

Activity

1 Why do you think the child might have decided to become a **vegetarian**? Explain to your partner what you think the parents felt about the child becoming a vegetarian.

2 Try to remember the first time that you made a decision that was different to your family or friends. How did you feel? Did you decide to give up something like the child in the poem?

Many religions have important ceremonies when people start to become a teenager. In some religions this confirms the faith that their parents may have dedicated them into when they were babies. Now is the time for the person themselves to make that decision and confirm for themselves their faith and beliefs.

There is always one moment in childhood when the door opens and lets the future in.

Graham Greene, writer, 1904–91

Bat Mitzvah

In Judaism, some girls around the age of twelve choose to have a **Bat Mitzvah**. In **Hebrew** the word 'bat' means 'daughter' and 'mitzvah' means '**commandment**'. This is seen as the girls entry into womanhood and she is seen to be responsible for observing the commandments. The ceremony will be the result of a lot of study about the religion and the importance of responsibilities to their family and to their religion. During the actual ceremony there will be religious readings and girls make a personal commitment to their beliefs.

When I had my Bat Mitzvah I felt so proud. I felt I was making a statement and standing up for what I believed in. None of my friends are Jewish and at times they thought I was stupid going to study Hebrew when I could have been going out. But I knew this was important to me.

Miriam

Many girls choose to celebrate their Bat Mitzvah in a way special to them. Stephanie Monty decided to 'twin' her Bat Mitzvah with Raquel Harstein and Hannah Marks who have severe learning difficulties. Stephanie's mother said 'we wanted Stephanie to understand that coming of age is not just about receiving but giving back and taking on responsibilities too. I think Stephanie has grown spiritually from it'.

Activity

Further activity

1 Imagine Miriam's friend has said:

> **Why don't you come out with us? No one else is having a Bat Mitzvah – what's the point?**

What do you think her reply would be?

2 Think of all the decisions you are going to make at some time of your life – decisions that are individual to you. What options to choose? Do you commit yourself to a religion? When will you marry? Where will you live? In a group, create a board game that will show the individual decisions each person may make in their life.

3 What do you think Stephanie's mother meant when she said 'I think Stephanie has grown spiritually'.

Making space for truth

Making space for what you believe in is very important. A Sikh story tells when **Guru Nanak Dev Ji** was travelling to a city to preach he was met by a messenger with a bowl of milk that was filled to the brim. The messenger said that people in the city did not want to give him space to teach about truth and goodness. The messenger said that just like a bowl of milk the city was full to overflowing and there would be no room for him.

Guru Nanak Dev Ji plucked a flower from a nearby branch and placed it on top of the milk. Amazingly the milk did not spill and as the flower floated the perfume could be smelt. The Guru told his listeners that there is always space for the influence of truth and goodness.

Thought diary

Can you remember a time when you did something that was important to you although your friends disapproved?

Key Words

Bat Mitzvah – *A girls coming of age at 12.*

Clones – *Identical copies.*

Commandment – *Order (from God).*

Guru Nanak Dev Ji – *The first Sikh Guru.*

Hebrew – *Language used by Jews for prayer and study.*

Vegetarian – *A person who does not eat meat or fish.*

Protecting our space

How would you feel if you came home to this? Or went out to play and found the park vandalized?

It does not matter where we live, we all depend on our surroundings and many of us feel we want to protect them. For many people their surroundings are part of their identity.

Activity

1 As you go home tonight, take a note of all the different examples of the ways that people have harmed your local environment. Think about the impact for people who live in that area.
Try to produce your findings in the form of a chain.
For example:

litter on the street ··> attracts rats ··> makes the street unsafe ··> makes the street look dirty

2 Who do you think the Earth belongs to? Remember to justify by giving a reason for your view.

Deforestation is resulting in the **extinction** of at least one species of bird, mammal or plant daily. Forests are being destroyed at the rate of one million acres (an area the size of Great Britain) each week!

Hindus are aware of how much humans depend on their surroundings and how important it is not to upset the natural balance of creation. Trees are seen as the most important example of plant life. Many Hindus consider trees as an example to follow in their lives. Trees grow slowly, creating an environment of peace and calm. Whenever a Hindu acts they should remember the importance of **ahimsa**, which means non-violence or non-harm. There are many different ways we can harm other people. What we say can sometimes be as hurtful as what we do.

The Chipko women

In the **Himalayas** many of the women thought of the forest as their friend. It provided them with firewood and food for their animals. The roots of the tree helped the earth to keep the rainwater.

Over the years, though, people saw the forest as a way to make money and started to cut down large areas of trees. In some areas, this deforestation has led to disaster, as heavy rain rushed down the bare hills causing floods and land-slides.

The Chipko women in the village of Gopeshwar heard that the Forestry Department were going to cut down 300 trees to make into sport equipment. They knew how much harder this would make their life. Without trees there was a greater risk of floods and less food for their animals. As Hindus, they knew that whatever action they took should be non-violent (ahimsa). After much thought, they decided to stage a protest by putting their arms around the trees to stop them from being cut down.

Activity

Further activity

1 Write down five ways a Hindu's belief in ahimsa might affect their thoughts or actions?

2 Create a banner for the Chipko women to use in their protest. Think carefully about a message they would want to write on the banner.

Thought diary

What space is so important to you that you would want to protect it? Explain why it is so important.

Key Words

Ahimsa – *Non-violence, respect for life.*
Deforestation – *Clearing of trees.*
Extinction – *No longer in existence.*
Himalayas – *Mountain range in Asia.*

Space for us all

Sometimes we consider our space as our own and no one else's.

That's my space!

Don't sit in my space!

Those boys shouldn't come here. This is our street – our space!

Activity

1 Using newspapers and magazines, make a collage to show how many disagreements happen because of space, the headline oppposite for example.

2 Now do the same again, but this time to show how a space can unite people.

REBEL ARMIES HAVE INVADED CAPITAL CITY

All religions teach that the land is not ours but is something that has been lent and should be treated well.

Christianity

Then the Lord God placed the man in the Garden of Eden to cultivate it and guard it.

Genesis 2: 15

Islam

Allah's trustees are responsible for maintaining the unity of his creation, its flora and fauna, its wildlife and natural environment.

The Muslim Declaration on Nature

Judaism

When God created the first human beings, God led them around the Garden of Eden and said: 'Look at my works! See how beautiful they are – how excellent! For your sake I created them all.'

Midrash Ecclesiastes Rabbah (First century)

Space used wisely can help unite people.

As well as having harmony with the land, it is important that we consider how the land can create harmony. Many people now are using spaces to try to create harmony between people of different religions or beliefs. In many schools there are reflection, or quiet rooms where pupils and staff can go. It does not matter if they belong to a religion or not, it is an area that unites people and gives them an opportunity to think about the bigger questions of life.

When we heard about the tragedy on September 11, lots of people from the school wanted to use the reflection room. There were pupils there who were Christians, Muslims, Jews, Hindus and people who do not believe in a God at all. It didn't matter what religion we were – we all were united.

Perhaps you would not think that a football pitch is being used as a space to try to create harmony between people. But the **Maimonides** Foundation has worked with Arsenal Football Club to try to promote friendship between Jews and Muslims in Great Britain. About 150 Muslim and Jewish children develop their football skills together in an atmosphere of trust and respect. The director of the Maimonides Foundation said:

Football is a common language across all the cultural divides. There's far more in common between Jews and Muslims than people know about. What's better than to start building relations at a very young level?

Activity

Further activity

1 Imagine you are the director of the Maimonides project trying to explain to Muslim and Jewish parents why it is important for their children to attend. What reasons might you give?

2 If your school was to have a reflection room, can you think about some rules you would want to make? Remember you want the space to unite people from different beliefs.

Thought diary

What spaces are around you where different types of people (for example, young and old) could meet together for a common aim?

Key Words

Maimonides – *An important Jewish religious teacher who lived 1135–1204 CE.*

Assessment

In this chapter we have begun to explore how we all need space to show our own identity and the important things in our lives.

Here are a few questions you might have thought about in each unit:

❶ *Space to be me – How is each person unique?*

❷ *Space to show the real me – How do people show their identity?*

❸ *Space to find me – Where do I go to think for myself?*

❹ *Space to show what I believe – Is it easy to believe different things to your friends and family?*

❺ *Protecting our space – How would I protect the space I am interdependent with?*

❻ *Space for us all – How can we use space to create harmony between people?*

Reflecting on your progress

❶ To help you reflect on what you have learnt from this chapter, look back on your work, or in your Thought diary, and write a few lines on each of the following areas, giving reasons to improve your answers:

ⓐ What I enjoyed. Why?
ⓑ What I found difficult. Why?

❷ Pick an idea that you had and try to explain it clearly to another person. Think about:

- Where the idea came from.
- What the idea is about.
- Why you like the idea.
- The *best* way to explain it to someone.

❸ In your Thought diary, copy down five **skills** that you have used during this chapter from the following list:

- I listened well to others.
- I gave reasons for my views.
- I expressed myself clearly.
- I tried to imagine other people's points of view.
- I developed my writing and artistic skills.
- I investigated a new topic by myself.
- I kept on task well.
- I used lots of imagination.
- I cared about the feelings of other people.
- I gave justified views.

❹ What facts did you learn? What do you understand now that you did not know about before? Make a spider diagram or a poster to show your thoughts.

Test yourself

❶ *When Anne Frank was in hiding she wrote in her diary*

> *Parents can only give good advice or put them on the right paths, but the final forming of a person's character lies in their own hands.*
>
> Anne Frank

Explain what you think the major influences are on someone's life? Do you think they change as they get older? Why? Give reasons for your thoughts.
[Level 4 – AT2]

❷ *How might belonging to a faith tradition make a difference to your identity? In your explanation you need to think about the effect it might have on the thoughts and actions of individual people. Try to give examples of when it might and might not.*
[Level 5 – AT2]

❸ *Imagine someone said to you 'Going on a retreat is just trying to escape from the real world'. Make a note of two points that are in favour of this view and two that are against. Select the view that you agree with most and write it as a detailed response.*
[Level 6 – AT2]

What next?

❶ *Look at the list of skills opposite. Choose two that you want to improve on in the future. Perhaps you could note them down in your Thought diary. (Describe two ways in which you could improve them. Is there someone who could give you suggestions? Is there some way of reminding yourself of your aims in future lessons?)*

❷ *Think about the topic you enjoyed most. What could you do to investigate it further? Are there any websites or books that could help you find out more?*

Well done!

You know more, have thought more and improved your skills. KEEP GOING! ✓

Ticking away

In this chapter you will consider the importance of reflecting upon and learning from the past by focusing on Christianity, Judaism and Buddhism.

What are you doing tonight? What are you looking forward to at the weekend? How will you celebrate your birthday? Where will you go on holiday? What options will you choose? What will you do when you leave school? There are so many important things to plan for and time is just ticking away. Sometimes we need to just STOP! Stop and think. Think about the past – our past. How has it helped to create us, the person we are today, and what are the lessons for the future?

Activity

1 Think about this time yesterday. Only yesterday, but 86,400 seconds ago!

  a What were you doing?

  b How did you feel?

  c What have you done since then?

  d What have you learnt since then?

  e How are you different?

2 So much has happened in one day in your life. What about the rest of the world? With a partner, note down a list of as many events that have happened in the past day. Make a note of them under the headings of:

- Local (your own area, including your school)
- National (the whole country)
- Global (anywhere in the rest of the world).

All religions consider it important to think about the future and the present, but they also think it is important to **reflect** upon the past. To reflect does not mean to be sad or miserable. It means to look back and consider. Just like the reflection in a mirror.

People may choose to reflect in many different ways. Sometimes people who belong to a faith might go to a place of worship and reflect on their own in silence.

Going into the church helps me think about the past. I feel closer to God, who has been my guide in the past and will be in the present.

Sometimes people prefer to go to a place where they can listen to music or look at pictures to bring back memories.

Somedays I go up to my bedroom, shut the door and get out my box of memories.

Many people throughout the world write diaries. These allow people a chance to reflect on important events that have happened and to record the special events or feelings of each day – just like your Thought diary.

Activity

Further activity

1 If you were going to create a box of memories, what would you put inside it? It can contain objects or special memories. Try to think of something to represent each year of your life.

2 Every person likes to reflect in their own place. For some people it is a place of worship or somewhere that is private. It might be sitting in the garden or lying on your bed. Think about your special place and either write about it or draw it.

3 Look at the list of words below and choose two that you feel when you are in your special place:

- peace
- calm
- lonely
- contented
- loved
- happy
- confused
- relaxed
- sad.

Thought diary

There are many questions you can answer that you could not answer a year ago. For many questions there are no easy answers. For some questions it may take a very long time to find answers – if you ever will.

What questions do you think you might still not be able to answer in 30 years time?

Key Words

Reflect – *To show or consider what something is like.*

A time to resolve

Have you ever stayed up until midnight on New Year's Eve? Did you notice the different moods of people? Many people feel excited about the New Year to come, but they also think about how they would like to change things. By looking at the past they learn and it helps them plan for the future. They **resolve** to do certain things – to make **resolutions** – then they have to work hard to achieve them and not give in to temptation!

As you begin your new topic it is a time to look back and reflect. Think back over your past year. Three hundred and sixty five days! So much will have happened in the world, in your school and to you.

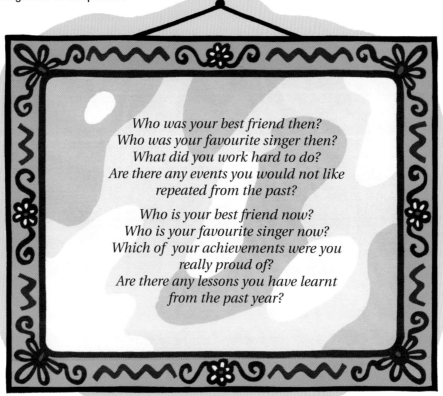

Who was your best friend then?
Who was your favourite singer then?
What did you work hard to do?
Are there any events you would not like repeated from the past?

Who is your best friend now?
Who is your favourite singer now?
Which of your achievements were you really proud of?
Are there any lessons you have learnt from the past year?

Activity

Draw two mirrors and label them A and B:

A will be for this time a year ago, and B will be for now, the present time.

In A write down the answers to the following questions:

- Who was your best friend then?
- Who was your favourite singer then?
- What did you work hard to do?
- Are there any events you would not like repeated from the past?

In B write down the answers to these questions:

- Who is your best friend now?
- Who is your favourite singer now?
- Which of your achievements were you really proud of?
- What important lessons have you learnt in the past year?

Resolutions are not like wishes that can magically happen. Usually people have to work hard so they are not tempted to break their resolutions. Some people have described **temptation** as a battle going on in the mind. In the end it is only you who can decide when to give in to temptation.

After Jesus was **baptized** in the **River Jordan**, he went into the wilderness. Here he wanted to reflect on what God wanted him to do. The devil tempted him three times. Each of the times Jesus resisted the temptation by remembering the teachings of the scriptures he had learnt.

Activity

Further activity

Look closely at the painting.

a Do you think the two angels were at the scene? If not, then why do you think the painter has included them?

b Why do you think Jesus appears so calm in the painting?

c Close your eyes and think of a time when you have been tempted. Try to remember what stopped you giving in to temptation.

If you are God's son, order these stones to turn into bread.

Throw yourself down from this high point of the Temple.

I will give you all the kingdoms of the world if you bow down and worship.

The scripture says, 'Man cannot live on bread alone, but needs every word that God speaks.'

The scripture also says, 'Do not put the Lord your God to the test.'

The scripture says, 'Worship the Lord your God and serve only him!'

This story shows that Jesus, like all human beings, was tempted during his life.

Thought diary

Over the next week make a note of all the ways you are tempted. Make a note of the reasons why you did or did not give in.

Key Words

Baptized – *Rite of initiation, immersing in or sprinkling of water.*

Resolutions – *Decisions of intentions of what you will do.*

Resolve – *To make up your mind; to promise yourself to do something.*

River Jordan – *River in Israel.*

Temptation – *Persuasion to do something.*

Past mistakes

We all do things we are sorry for, so why do we find it so hard to own up? Is it because we are not brave enough? Or does there never seem to be the right time or the right person? Is it easier to try to forget the wrong things we have done and just start again? In this unit we will explore how some Christians show they are sorry for their wrongdoings.

Activity

1 If you were Amy what would you do? Look at the list below and choose one of the actions. Make sure you have justified your decision.

- Do not tell Karen what you have done, but buy her chocolates as a surprise present.
- Tell Karen what you have done and ask her to forgive you.
- Tell a friend to tell Karen that you are sorry.

- Do not tell Karen and do not mention it again.
- Write Karen a letter admitting what you have done.
- Try to forget it.

2 If you did chose to try to forget it, could your friendship ever be the same?

Justify your answer by giving a reason.

Forgiveness does not mean ignoring what has been done or putting a false label on an evil act. It means, rather, that the evil act no longer remains a barrier to the relationship.

Strength to Love, Martin Luther King

Being sorry for your wrong actions and thoughts is an important part of Christian life. Most Christians believe that wrong actions separate people from God, so before they worship they seek his forgiveness. In some Churches, people **confess** their wrongdoings as they pray. This happens in many **denominations**. In Salvation Army **citadels** there is a seat at the front of the building where people can kneel to ask for God's forgiveness. This seat is called the **mercy** seat.

In some Churches, such as the Roman Catholic Church, people confess their sins to a priest. He will act as God's representative and will tell them ways they can show they are truly sorry for their actions. The priest is not allowed to tell anyone else what they have been told and often does not know who the person is. In many Roman Catholic churches there is a **confessional box** with a curtain separating the priest from the person confessing. In some churches there is a **reconciliation** room where the person confessing and the priest sit in view of each other. Some Christians prefer this as they feel it makes a more friendly and relaxed setting.

Activity

Further activity

1 Explain in your own words why you think Christians believe that wrong actions separate people from God.

2 How do you think making a confession might help someone?

3 What qualities do you think a priest would need to have to hear confessions?

4 Imagine the class was going to interview a priest about confession. Think of three questions you would like to ask him. Discuss your questions with a partner and try to decide what answers the priest might give.

Thought diary

Who do you tell when you have done wrong things? How do you feel afterwards? Is there a difference in how you feel before and afterwards?

Key Words

Citadels – *Places of worship for members of the Salvation Army.*

Confess – *To say you have done something wrong.*

Confessional box – *Small room in which a person asks for forgiveness for their sins in the presence of a priest.*

Denomination – *Branch of the Christian Church.*

Mercy – *Not to harm or punish.*

Reconciliation – *Offering forgiveness of sins.*

Reflecting on the past

Close your eyes and think back to the last year. Try to think of all those times when you know you made people happy. How did you feel?

Now can you remember a time when you know you made someone unhappy? It might have been something you said or did, or even something you did not do! Did you show that person you were sorry for hurting them?

Sometimes we read in the newspapers of families and friends not speaking for years. Often they cannot even remember what the disagreement was about.

In Judaism, the New Year is called **Rosh Hashanah** and it is a time when Jews look forward to making a fresh start in the next year. It is also a time to look back and reflect on their behaviour during the past year. Many Jews believe that during the ten days between Rosh Hashanah and **Yom Kippur** (the Day of Atonement) God will open the Book of Life to look at the actions of each person during the year. During the next ten days each person has a chance to ask for forgiveness and 'wipe out' some of the wrongdoings before the book is closed for the year. It's up to them whether they take that chance.

Blowing the shofar at the western wall in israel

At the **synagogue** the **shofar** will be blown. This is a musical instrument made from a ram's horn. It is sounded one hundred times and acts as an alarm bell to remind Jews that God is present and to reflect on all they may have done wrong.

Often Jews will then go to a place where there is flowing water. Here they will empty their pockets of any crumbs into the water. This reminds them that they too can be emptied of all their wrongdoings before the start of the New Year.

Activity

1 Explain how the shofar acts as an alarm clock.

2 What makes you aware that you have done wrong things?

3 Why do you think some Jews go to running water to empty their pockets?

The ten days between Rosh Hashanah and the holiest day of Yom Kippur are called the ten days of return or **repentance**. This time gives Jews a chance to repent for all the wrong they may have done and the people they may have hurt. Jewish people believe God can forgive the broken promises people have made to Him, but it is only the people they have wronged who can forgive for those actions.

> *To a person who says: 'I will sin and repent', the Day of **Atonement** brings no forgiveness. For sins against God, the Day of Atonement brings forgiveness. But for sins against one's neighbour, the Day of Atonement brings no forgiveness until he has become reconciled with his neighbour.*
>
> The **Talmud**

The first step is admitting to a mistake and then thinking of ways to make up for it. This does not mean just saying you are sorry but showing you are and making sure you do not let it happen again. Jews can then make a new beginning, and on Yom Kippur they can spend the day asking God for forgiveness for the things they have done wrong against him.

Activity

Further activity

1 Is it a good idea to have a time of year when everyone reflects on the past year and asks for forgiveness before the start of a new year? You need to give a reason for and against.

2 Devise a Rosh Hashanah greeting card. On your card try to show how you would express the theme of forgiveness.

Thought diary

Do you think that every wrongdoing can be forgiven? Are there some actions which can never be forgiven?

Key Words

Atonement – *Coming back to God after doing wrong.*

Repentance – *To show that you regret.*

Rosh Hashanah – *The ten-day festival for New Year in Judaism.*

Shofar – *Ram's horn blown during Rosh Hashanah.*

Synagogue – *A place of worship for Jews.*

Talmud – *Book containing the ancient Jewish ceremonies and civil laws.*

Yom Kippur – *The holiest day of the year for Jews at the end of the ten days of Rosh Hashanah. Also called the Day of Atonement.*

Lessons from the past

Who have you learnt from? Every one of us has been influenced by someone else. It might be because they had a particular skill we admire or because they showed great courage. Their influence might last for a few weeks or months, or the whole of a lifetime. Usually we show respect for these people in our memories but sometimes there are other ways.

MOTHER TERESA'S HOSPICE

NELSON MANDELA DRIVE

ANNE FRANK DAY

HAPPY St PATRICK'S DAY

BREAKTHROUGH ON PARKINSON'S DISEASE

Monument to Gandhi in Eusten gardens

Tree of life with name plates in a synagogue

Activity

1 With a partner, list the ways that we remember the life, actions or teachings of people who have lived before us.

2 You have three minutes to jot down a list of twenty people who are famous today. Now compare your list with your partner's. Discuss how many of the people on your list you think will still be famous in twenty years' time.

3 Interview five people of different ages. Find out the name of the person they admire. How do they show they respect them?

A Buddhist view

Buddhists do not consider the **Buddha** as a God, but as a special human being who became **enlightened** – that is, he came to understand the truth about life. During his life he gave many teachings. Although he lived about 2,500 years ago, many people today try to follow what he taught.

Each year Buddhists have a special day called **Wesak**, or Buddha Day, when they honour the life of the Buddha. It was on this day that the Buddha was born, became enlightened and died. During the day, Buddhists listen to stories and lectures on the life of the Buddha, and put into practice his teachings by showing kindness and giving to charity. In some countries, Buddhists walk around a monastery three times and remember the life of the Buddha, the **Dharma** (teachings of the Buddha), and the **Sangha** (community of Buddhists).

Activity

Further activity

1 Why do you think light is used as a symbol at Wesak? Can you think of any other symbols that are used at festivals?

2 With your partner, think of five questions you might want to ask the Buddha to help you find the truth about life.

Thought diary

Who has had the most influence on the way you think, act and believe?

Key Words

Buddha – *The enlightened one.*
Dharma – *The teachings of the Buddha.*
Enlightened – *To understand the truth about life.*
Sangha – *The Buddhist community.*
Wesak – *Festival for the Buddha's birth, enlightenment and death.*

Learning the hard way

We all make mistakes. The good thing about making mistakes is learning from them! It is not just our own mistakes we need to learn from. When we reflect on all that is going on in the world today, we realize we have a lot of lessons to learn.

Activity

Think about your own life. Try to remember times when you have learnt from your past mistakes.

Perhaps you can remember a time when you ate so much you felt ill? Or a time when you put your hand into a flame and got burnt?

Hiroshima

On a bright sunny day on 6 August 1945, the United States dropped an **atom** bomb on the Japanese city of Hiroshima. This was the first time that a **nuclear** weapon had ever been used. There was immediate disaster.

Toge Mitsuyoshi saw the bomb dropping:

How could I ever forget that flash of light! In a moment thirty thousand people ceased to be.

The suffering did not end there. The effects remained as the atom bomb had filled the air with **radiation** – a kind of poison that stays inside people for a long time, sometimes forever. Sadako was only two years old when the bomb dropped. She was a happy Buddhist girl who was very good at running. One day while she was running she began to feel dizzy. Her parents took her to a hospital where they were told she had a sickness called **leukaemia** which was caused by the bomb.

While she was ill her friend brought her a golden crane as a good-luck charm. Sadako aimed to make 1,000 cranes, believing she would get well if she did so. Everyone saved paper for her. Gradually, as the months

Atomic bomb mushroom cloud

passed by, Sadako became weaker and weaker but still carried on making her cranes.

On 25 October 1955, Sadako died – ten years after the bomb was dropped. Sadako had made 664 cranes. After Sadako's death her friends folded 336 cranes so that 1,000 could be placed with Sadako.

Sadako's friends began to dream of creating a monument to her and all the children who were killed by the atom bomb. They thought it was important that people remembered the lessons of the past and how the effects of war can last such a long time. In 1958, the statue was unveiled in the Hiroshima Peace Park. It is a representation of Sadako holding a golden crane in outstretched hands.

Paper cranes are placed beneath it. On the base of the statue it says:

This is our cry
This is our prayer
Peace in the world.

To remember the past
Is to commit oneself to the future.
To remember Hiroshima
Is to abhor nuclear war.

Pope John Paul II

Activity

Further activity

1 Using your own words, explain how you think the statue of Sadako would remind people about the importance of peace.

2 With your partner, brainstorm a list of events which you think should never happen again.

3 Look through a range of newspapers and magazines and make a collage to show how we are learning from past events, for example, global warning, or that smoking can cause cancer.

Thought diary

How do you think you could 'commit yourself to the future'? What could you do that could be important for future generations?

Key Words

Atom – *The smallest part of an element that can take place in a chemical reaction.*

Leukaemia – *Serious illness which affects the blood.*

Nuclear – *Weapons that explode using the energy released by atoms.*

Radiation – *Stream of particles given out by a radioactive substance.*

Sadako's statue in Hiroshima peace park

Assessment

In this chapter we have begun to explore the importance of looking back at the past – not just in our own lives, but for the whole world.

> *Who controls the past controls the future.*
>
> George Orwell (1903–53), writer

Here are a few questions that you might have thought about in each unit:

❶ *Ticking away – Where do you go to reflect on the past?*

❷ *A time to resolve – How do you resist temptation?*

❸ *Past mistakes – Why is it hard to say sorry?*

❹ *Reflecting on the past – Is it easier to forgive or forget?*

❺ *Lessons from the past – How do we remember people who have inspired us?*

❻ *Learning the hard way – Why is it important to learn from the past?*

Reflecting on your progress

❶ To help you reflect on what you have learnt from this chapter, look back on your work, or in your Thought diary, and write a few lines on each of the following areas, giving reasons to improve your answers:

    ⓐ What I enjoyed. Why?

    ⓑ What I found difficult. Why?

❷ Pick an idea that you had and try to explain it clearly to another person. Think about:

- Where the idea came from.
- What the idea is about.
- Why you like the idea.
- The *best* way to explain it to someone.

❸ In your Thought diary, copy down five **skills** that you have used during this chapter from the following list:

- I listened well to others.
- I gave reasons for my views.
- I expressed myself clearly.
- I tried to imagine other people's points of view.
- I developed my writing and artistic skills.
- I investigated a new topic by myself.
- I kept on task well.
- I used lots of imagination.
- I cared about the feelings of other people.
- I gave justified views.

❹ What facts did you learn? What do you understand now that you did not know about before? Make a spider diagram or a poster to show your thoughts.

Test yourself

❶ *Do you think it is important to have a time of year when you can reflect on the past? Give two reasons or justifications for your view. [Level 3 – AT2]*

❷ *'Memories should be kept in your head. You do not need statues to help you remember.' Do you agree with this comment? Explain one reason for the comment and one against. [Level 4 – AT2]*

❸ *Think of someone who you really admire for the work they have done. Imagine you have been put in charge of organizing a memorial for them. It can be any sort of memorial you want, a statue, a special event, a poster – it's up to you. What would you consider to be a good way to reflect their work? You will need to include:*

- *who you would choose and why*
- *why you think their work/life should be remembered*
- *what memorial would reflect their importance*
- *what special symbols or music you would use and why.*

Remember to think about relevant symbols, colours, inscriptions and where it would be. [Level 6 – AT2]

❹ *We learn important lessons every day of our lives. Sometimes we are taught them by someone, sometimes it is our own experiences from which we learn. What is the most important lesson you have learnt in your life? In your answer try to explain when it happened and the effect it will have on the rest of your life. [Level 6 – AT2]*

Where next?

❶ *Look at the list of skills opposite. Choose two that you want to improve on in the future. Perhaps you could note them down in your Thought diary. (Describe two ways in which you could improve them. Is there someone who could give you suggestions? Is there some way of reminding yourself of your aims in future lessons?)*

❷ *Think about the topic you enjoyed most. What could you do to investigate it further? Are there any websites or books that could help you find out more?*

Well done!

You know more, have thought more and improved your skills. KEEP GOING! ✔

Communication without words

In this chapter you will consider what communication is and whether it is easy. You will also consider how pictures communicate ideas to us, how we know the truth and how people may communicate with God by focusing on Buddhism, Islam and Christianity.

Communication is a key part of our everyday lives, something we take for granted. We communicate in lots of different ways with people; it is not just about the things we say. **Body language**, facial expressions, the way we dress, the way we walk and the things we enjoy – all communicate something about us to other people.

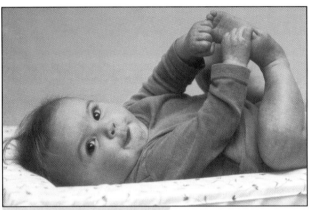

How do we communicate with babies?

The less you talk, the more you are listened to.

Abigail van Buren

Activity

1 How do babies tell their parents what they want?

2 Can you remember how you told your parents that you were hungry, or that you did not like a certain food?

3 How do you think you learned to talk?

There is a theory that we learn by example. When we are born we are **socialized** into behaving in particular ways. Akbar, the emperor of India from 1542 to 1605ce, believed children would learn to speak to God in **Hebrew**

without being taught! He had his children raised by servants who could not hear or speak. The children did not learn to speak Hebrew, but they did learn to communicate using gestures.

Imagine what your life would be like if you could no longer communicate using speech.

● Make a list of the difficulties you would face each day.

● How would it feel if you could no longer hear or see? What difficulties might you face then?

Helen Keller was born in America in 1880. When she was 19 months old, she became ill and as a result was left blind and deaf. It was Alexander Graham Bell, the

Helen Keller

inventor of the telephone, who helped Helen's parents find a teacher for her. Helen was taught how to spell words with her fingers, and eventually she learned to write. Her work became famous and although her desire to speak was never realized, she was invited to lecture across America. Her teacher, Anne Sullivan Macy, interpreted her sounds and addressed questions from the crowd to Helen.

Through Anne, Helen was able to speak to the world.

The public must realize that the blind man is neither genius or freak, nor an idiot. He has a mind that can be educated, a hand that can be trained, ambitions which it is right for him to strive to realize, and it is the duty of the public to help him make the best of himself so that he can win light through work.

Helen said:

What do you understand by the phrase 'win light through work'?

The best and most beautiful things in the world cannot be seen or even touched. They must be felt by the human heart.

She also said:

What did Helen Keller mean by 'the best and most beautiful things in the world'? Can you give some examples?

Does the human heart feel things? Is it a part of our communication system? Explain your thoughts.

Thought diary

You have considered how we communicate and what we communicate. Jot down some thoughts about the things you think need to be communicated to people in the world today.

How could you best do this?

Key Words

Body language – *The way you move and gesture, and what it communicates to other people.*

Hebrew – *An ancient language still spoken by some people today.*

Socialized – *To mix socially with others.*

Activity

Further activity

Not everyone understands the things we try to communicate. In Jostein Gaarder's book, *Through a Glass Darkly*, the angel, Ariel, throws a snowball to Cecilia and tells her that he has never felt snow. She says to Ariel:

'You must be joking! You've just felt it.'

'I didn't feel anything. Angels don't feel anything, Cecilia.'

'Didn't you feel that it was cold?

He had a resigned expression.

'You really must learn these things. If you don't, it won't be much fun talking to you. Feeling a snowball is the same for us as feeling a thought. You can't feel the memory of the snow that fell last year.'

She shook her head, and Ariel asked, 'How does it feel to hold a snowball?'

'Cold – ice cold.'

'You've said that already.'

Now she had to try hard.

'Your skin tingles. It tingles like strong peppermints. You want to take your hand away and shiver. But it's lovely all the same.'

Ariel had leaned over inquisitively as she spoke. 'I've never tasted peppermint,' he said. 'I've never shivered either.'

Think about how Ariel must have felt not knowing how snow feels. Now imagine you have to communicate the feelings in the list below to aliens from outer space. How would you do it? Would you use words or pictures?

a Happiness
b Love
c Sadness
d Togetherness.

Freedom of speech

People try to communicate effectively with the world and with each other. In the United Kingdom we are very lucky and can say what we want. This is known as having freedom of speech. Not everyone is as fortunate as us. Read the extract below from **Amnesty International**.

Nafiji was arrested with three of her friends because they formed a 'Freedom Society' to protest when Albanian languages were stopped at their school. In the trial, the court was given evidence that Nafiji had done well at school and had no record of anti-social behaviour. But she was still sentenced to four years in prison. Nafiji was released six months after Amnesty International took up her case. Her friends are still in prison.

Activity

1 Having read the extract, do you think that what happened to Nafiji and her friends was fair? Explain your answer.

2 Imagine that you want to express an opinion about something that happened in school. It might be that you do not like school dinners, or that you would like to have more choice about the subjects you do in school. Would you be punished for expressing your views? Would the head teacher expel you? Would you be arrested?

A Buddhist perspective

In many countries around the world people have to be careful about the things they say, do, write and believe. There are countries where governments do not approve of people holding particular opinions or following a particular religion.

Tibet is one country where people have suffered and been unable to follow their spiritual leader, the **Dalai Lama**. The Dalai Lama was persuaded to sign an agreement with China in 1949 when he was only 15 years old. The agreement stated that Tibet was really a part of China but that the Chinese Government would not try to influence or change the religion or culture of the Tibetan people. The Chinese Government did not keep their word and they invaded Tibet, taking homes and forcing the farmers to grow different crops. As a result, hunger became widespread as food shortages grew. Children were no longer allowed to learn about Tibet in school and lessons were taught in Chinese.

Buddhism teaches non-violence and the Dalai Lama told the people of Tibet not to use force in their fight against the Chinese army. He and other Buddhists were forced to escape and set up a refuge in India. They still care for the people of Tibet. He has set in place plans to try to help people, always without the idea of violence. The Dalai Lama is admired and respected throughout the world, and was awarded the **Nobel Peace Prize** in 1989.

He said:

> *All religions can work together despite fundamental difference in philosophy. Every religion aims at serving humanity. Therefore it is possible to work together to serve humanity and contribute to world peace.*

In 1996 the Chinese Government banned the people of Tibet from carrying pictures of the Dalai Lama.

Should people have the right to practise their own religion without people arresting them? Do you think that religious people of the world today could learn from the statement made by the Dalai Lama? If so, what could they learn?

Activity

Further activity

1 Imagine you are living in a country where, if you communicated your thoughts, you could be arrested. You are told what to think about life, love and the universe by the ruling power. To communicate your disagreement could cost you your life. Jot down some thoughts about how this would make you feel. Share your ideas with a partner.

2 We are lucky to live in a country where communication is fairly free. Communication allows us access to so much information. We have telephones that let us say what we want, teachers who listen, and **media** that allows us access to material about world wide events.

How different would your life be without these methods of communication?

3 Design a poster/collage communicating the idea of freedom, such as the freedom to express an opinion or believe in a religion.

4 Try to find out about the United Nations Declaration of Human Rights.

Thought diary

Having considered the consequences of not having the freedom to communicate, do you think communication is important? Explain your thoughts.

Is communication the only important thing in life? Make a list of the things you think are important in your life. Consider whether you take these things for granted.

Key Words

Amnesty International – *An organization that works to help people who are imprisoned wrongly.*

Dalai Lama – *Spiritual leader of the Tibetan people.*

Media – *A general word covering TV, newspapers, magazines, books, CDs and the Internet.*

Nobel Peace Prize – *A prize awarded to people who do great things.*

Every picture tells a story

Sometimes words are just not enough when we want to say something to people. Imagine a friend who is crying and needs some comfort; words may not be enough to make them feel better, but a hug can make a huge difference.

There is a saying that a picture can speak louder than a thousand words. It is very true. The news has often used images and pictures to convey scenes where people are hurt, hungry and upset.

Here are some examples of images used in the media.

Activity

1 Look at these pictures and jot down what you think each one is trying to communicate.

2 Why do you think these pictures have been used in the media?

3 Can pictures be more effective than words? Why? Share your thoughts with a partner. Do you agree with each other?

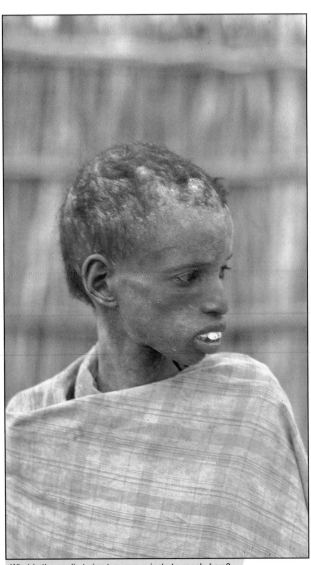

What is the media trying to communicate to people here?

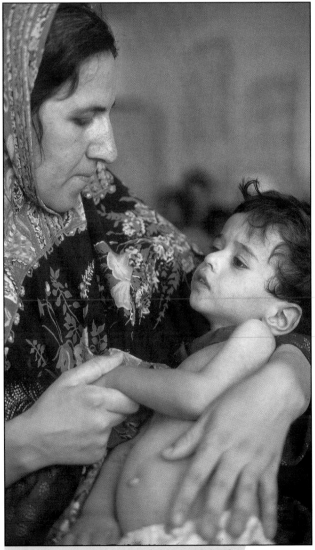

What is the media trying to communicate to people here?

Pictures are often used in religion to illustrate something that has happened in the history of the religion and some important religious beliefs.

Here are some examples of religious art. Look closely at each picture, and with a partner try to work out what each picture is telling you. Look at how colour is used, and expressions on peoples faces. What does the picture tell you about the people who painted it and where they lived?

- What story do you think is being told in each picture?
- If you had to draw a picture to communicate something about your family, what would you draw?

Ganesha

Krishna teaching Arjuna

Rama and Hanuman

Activity

Further activity

Take a story from any religious tradition that you are familiar with – it can be anything you like. With a partner, design a picture or a scene that can tell the story or part of the story.

Thought diary

Pictures and images can say a lot about who we are and the person we want to be. Think about who you are, the things you do well, colours that reflect your personality, and elements of nature that might represent you. Try to sketch a symbol, shape or image that would reflect you.

Communication with God

*God, 'a being than which nothing greater can be **conceived**'.*

St Augustine, talking about the Christian idea of God

In many religious traditions belief in God is absolutely central. Beliefs about God can be unchanging and have to be passed on from generation to generation. These beliefs about God are part of the tradition itself and are reflected in worship and behaviour.

In the religion of **Islam**, **Muslims** worship Allah (God.) They believe Allah has lots of great qualities, but you will never see any artists' impressions of Allah or His chosen prophet, **Muhammad (pbuh)**. Why do you think this might be?

Instead, in Islam, names are given to Allah. He has '99 beautiful names' that are written in Arabic. These are displayed in mosques, the Muslim place of worship, using calligraphy. These words remind Muslims of how great Allah is and why He is worthy of worship.

Some of the 99 beautiful names are displayed below.

The Merciful One
The Compassionate
The Almighty
The Creator
The Hearer
He Who Sees
He Who Pardons
The Powerful
The Generous
The Wise
The Loving One
The Provider
The Judge
The Well Informed
The Life Giver
The Light

Activity

1 With a partner, read through the list of Allah's names and try to work out what these names communicate to people about the nature of Allah.

2 Why might these names have been given to Allah? Choose three and try to find out about what they refer to.

3 How might these beliefs affect how Muslims behave? Explain your thoughts. Think about how they might feel about the end of life, the foods they eat and how they treat the world and each other.

The five pillars of Islam

Muslims remind themselves every day of their faith in Allah. They do this by following the **shahadah**. This is one of the five key beliefs of Islam, one of the five pillars of Islam.

The five pillars of Islam are:

- Shahadah – the declaration of belief that there is one God and that Muhammad (pbuh) is His messenger.
- Salah – praying five times a day.
- Zakah – paying 2.5 per cent of your earnings to help the needy.
- Sawm – fasting during the month of Ramadan.
- Hajj – making a pilgrimage to the holy city of Makkah.

The shahadah is said first thing in the morning and last thing at night, whispered into a newborn baby's ear and into the ear of someone who is dying. It states that:

There is only one God, Allah, and Muhammad (pbuh) was his prophet.

Shahadah – the Muslim declaration of faith

Activity

Further activity

1 Why do you think Muslims start and end their lives and start and end each day by saying the shahadah?

2 If you had to remind yourself of something every day, something that is important about how to live your life – what would you say?

3 How do the five pillars of Islam relate to communication with God?

Thought diary

We often give people names without really thinking about how much we know that person. When we do this it can lead to **stereotyping** people. This means we put a 'label' on someone and try to put them in a 'box'.

Can you think of any names we sometimes give to people? Are these good or bad names? How might 'labelling' someone affect them? Jot down some thoughts on these questions.

Key Words

Conceived – *To have an idea or opinion.*

Islam – *Devotion or willingness to surrender to the will of Allah.*

Muhammad (pbuh) – *The prophet of Islam.*

Muslims – *People devoted to Allah.*

Shahadah – *The first pillar of Islam.*

Stereotype – *A person or thing that represents a type.*

Communication and religion

Religions from around the world try to teach us about how we should behave, how we should approach life and the situations we face each day.

The lessons religions teach are seen to be very important. They reflect something about life, how important and how precious it is, and how we should not take it for granted.

People today, religious or not, believe that even though some of the rules taught by the religious founders were made thousands of years ago, we can still learn from them today.

Rather than giving people a list of rules to learn and follow, stories about the leaders of the religion, or parables that they told, are used to illustrate just how we should behave in life. Many religious leaders led by example and people today can learn from the things they did in their lives.

Activity

1 Do you think human life is important? Why?

2 Does the way people behave today show that they think human life is important?

Here is a story about the man who became known as the Buddha. Read the story carefully.

The man who became the Buddha

Prince **Siddhartha Gautama** lived what many would call an ideal life. He had a beautiful wife, a healthy son, and a loving family. He had lived inside his palace all his life and had never seen unpleasantness, poverty or sickness.

The Prince, however, was becoming bored with his life and wanted more. He told his chariot driver to take him out for a drive. On the journey he saw an old person, a sick person and a funeral. The Prince was shocked; he had not seen these sides of life before. He then saw a homeless monk who relied on the generosity of others for food. The monk was content with his life.

These things made the Prince think, and he decided to leave the palace and go in search of true happiness.

During his search, he tried lots of different methods to discover true happiness. He lived off a grain of rice a day and he meditated for long periods of time. Through his experiences, he found that the answer lay in the 'Middle Way'. This meant that people should not live a life of luxury nor should they live a life without the basic things everybody needs to live a decent life.

Activity

Further activity

1 Make a list of all the things that can be learned from the story.

   a Do these points mean anything for life today?

   b Are stories a good way to communicate lessons about life? Why?

2 Can you think of a story you have been told that made you think about life? What was the story?

3 All religions teach the idea that people should treat others how they themselves would want to be treated. This idea reflects the belief that we are all equal regardless of race, colour or belief.

   With a partner, write a story to tell to younger children in primary school. The story has to reflect the idea that all people are equal and should be treated the same. How are you going to do this? What story are you going to tell?

   You need to think about the language you use, the characters in the story and how you are going to present it. The story will be printed out using computers and then sent to the local school.

Thought diary

Buddhism tries to communicate how life should be lived. Think about how people live their lives today. Do you think if people followed the teachings of the Buddha life could be improved at all? Explain your answer with examples.

Key Words

Siddhartha Gautama – *The man who founded Buddhism. He left everything he had to find the answers to questions about life.*

Communicating truth

> **'I'm telling you the truth.'**

How often have we heard this statement? What does it really mean?

Activity

1 In pairs, try to work out what we what we mean when we say something is true. Do we have to be able to prove a statement for it to be true?

2 Lots of things we read about in the news can make us ask questions about whether or not something is true. Look at the following statements, and, in pairs, try to decide whether or not they are true.

- David Beckham is the best footballer ever.
- The symbol for water is H_2O.
- Chocolate does not make you fat.
- The world came about after the 'Big Bang'.
- The Beatles were a brilliant band.
- Newspapers always tell the truth.
- God is real.
- *Neighbours* is shown on BBC1.

Which statements did you decide were true? How do you know they are true? Discuss your thinking.

3 It can be difficult to say what is true. There are some things that all people agree on as being true, such as 'water evaporates when it boils'. However, there are lots of other things that some people believe to be true that other people would disagree with. An example of such a statement could be, 'killing animals is wrong'.

In pairs, make a list of other statements that some people believe to be true, which other people would disagree with. Why do some people believe such statements are true? Do they have any evidence to support their claims?

Religious people have beliefs and convictions about God that they believe to be true. These are laid down in holy books.

Some people believe stories told in the holy books are **literally true**. This means they believe that these events actually happened. Other people believe that these stories, whether factually true or not, are important because they can tell us something crucial about human life.

Read this story from the Old Testament in the Bible about Daniel.

Daniel was seen as someone very important by the king and he was given power over the kingdom. Other members of the king's government were jealous of him. They wanted to get rid of Daniel and told the king that there should be a new law introduced. Anyone who worshipped anyone other than the king was to be thrown to the lions!

Daniel was caught worshipping God and sentenced according to the law. The king was sad to see Daniel go and secretly hoped God would save him. The jealous ministers in the government were delighted to see an end to Daniel.

However, the next morning they went to see what remained of his body, only to see Daniel sitting in the lions' den alive, in one piece and unhurt! They were amazed.

Daniel explained that an angel had been sent from God to protect him. The king was delighted to have his adviser back with him and sent his other advisers to the lions!

Daniel: 6

Activity

1 What is the message of the story of Daniel?

2 Does it matter whether or not it is true?

3 If it is not true, can it still communicate some truth to the reader?

Communicating beliefs about life after death

Religions communicate their beliefs to their followers in many different ways and beliefs about what happens when you die are as important as any other. For lots of people their belief centres on the idea that what you do during your life on earth can affect what happens to you after death. Religious leaders believe it is very important to communicate beliefs about what happens after death.

There is no single belief about what happens after death, but there are lots of ideas about what could happen.

In Christianity and Islam there is the idea of Heaven and Hell. If you live a good life and follow God or Allah's teachings, you will go to Heaven; if not you will go to Hell. Jewish people have a slightly different view and believe that when you die your soul goes to the place of the dead.

Sikhs and Hindus believe in **reincarnation**. This means that after death you are reborn, able to live another life. The life you are reborn into is dependent on the life you have left. If you have lived a good life, you will get a good rebirth. If you have lived a bad life, you will get a bad rebirth.

Buddhists have similar ideas, believing that how you live your life now affects how your life-force is reborn.

Activity

Further activity

1 Can we know whether beliefs about life after death are true or not?

2 Do you think that one group of people have got the right answer or do you think that there is no right answer to the question 'what happens when you die'?

3 What do you believe happens when you die? Give reasons for your answer.

Thought diary

Thinking about the idea of truth, make a list of five things in your life you know to be true. Then consider how you know these things are true. How do you communicate these ideas to other people? Does it matter if they do not see these ideas as true?

Key Words

Literally true – *If a person believes a book is literally true, they believe that the events in the book actually took place as they are described – so some people believe that God made the world in six days and each day lasted 24 hours.*

Reincarnation – *The idea that after death you are reborn to live another life.*

Assessment

In this unit we have been thinking about just how people communicate with each other and with God. You have learnt that there are lots of different ways in which people can communicate and have also considered whether beliefs need to be true or not to be of value.

What is this picture telling you?

Here are a few questions that you might have thought about in each unit:

❶ *Communication without words – What do we mean when we talk about communication?*

❷ *Freedom of speech – Is communication always free and easy?*

❸ *Every picture tells a story – How do the media communicate with us?*

A litter mountain

❹ *Communication with God – How do people communicate with God?*

❺ *Communication and religion – What important lessons can we learn from religion?*

❻ *Communicating truth – How do you know if something is true or not?*

Reflecting on your progress

❶ To help you reflect on what you have learnt from this chapter, look back on your work, or in your Thought diary, and write a few lines on each of the following areas, giving reasons to improve your answers:

ⓐ What I enjoyed. Why?

ⓑ What I found difficult. Why?

❷ Pick an idea that you had and try to explain it clearly to another person. Think about:

- Where the idea came from.
- What the idea is about.
- Why you like the idea.
- The *best* way to explain it to someone.

❸ In your Thought diary, copy down five **skills** that you have used during this chapter from the following list:

- I listened well to others.
- I gave reasons for my views.
- I expressed myself clearly.
- I tried to imagine other people's points of view.
- I developed my writing and artistic skills.
- I investigated a new topic by myself.
- I kept on task well.
- I used lots of imagination.
- I cared about the feelings of other people.
- I gave justified views.

❹ What facts did you learn? What do you understand now that you did not know about before? Make a spider diagram or a poster to show your thoughts.

Test yourself

❶ *How do people communicate their ideas about God? Give at least two examples and try to include more than one religious tradition. [Level 4 – AT1]*

❷ *Can pictures and symbols be used effectively to communicate ideas and beliefs? Use examples in your answer and give reasons for your thoughts. [Level 5 – AT1]*

❸ *'Religious stories are a load of rubbish! They have nothing to tell us about what we should do today!' What do you think about this viewpoint? Explain your answer, giving examples from different traditions. Try to write at least ten lines. [Level 6 – AT2]*

What next?

❶ *Look at the list of skills opposite. Choose two that you want to improve on in the future. Perhaps you could note them down in your Thought diary. (Describe two ways in which you could improve them. Is there someone who could give you suggestions? Is there some way of reminding yourself of your aims in future lessons?)*

❷ *Think about the topic you enjoyed most. What could you do to investigate it further? Are there any websites or books that could help you find out more?*

Well done!

You know more, have thought more and improved your skills. KEEP GOING! ✓

Christianity key facts

Christianity – what is it?

Where and when did it begin?

Palestine, a part of the Roman Empire, now Israel. Jesus born between 6 and 4 BCE; religion began after his death approximately 29 CE.

Who founded it?

Jesus Christ (title from the Greek meaning 'Messiah', a Hebrew title meaning 'chosen by God').

Followers

Known as disciples (meaning 'followers') particularly twelve Apostles (meaning 'messengers') who were Jesus's closest companions: Simon (who later became known as Peter), his brother Andrew, James, John, Philip, Bartholomew, Thomas, Matthew, James son of Alphaeus, Thaddaeus, Simon the Zealot and Judas Iscariot.

Special writings

The Bible is made up of 66 books, 39 of which were written before Jesus and 27 of which were by followers after his death. These sections are known as 'Testaments' meaning 'agreement'. The Roman Catholics include a further section called The Apocrypha, literature covering the period of history between the writing of the Old and New Testaments. Some Christians believe that the Bible contains the unaltered word of God and literally believe every word. Other Christians believe that, although the Bible is inspired by God, it was written by people and is therefore open to error.

Symbol

The Christian cross.

Places of worship

Christians usually meet for regular worship on Sundays, the day on which they remember the resurrection of Jesus. The central part of this worship for most Christians is the Eucharist, meaning 'thanksgiving'; an event remembering the last meal that Jesus shared with his disciples on earth in which he broke bread and shared wine saying that these elements were his body and blood. Christians share this meal together in memory of Jesus's sacrifice on the cross. Worship can take different forms but usually involves readings from the Bible, prayers, hymns of praise and a sermon from the person leading the service, who may be a priest or vicar.

Pilgrimages

There are many sites of pilgrimages for Christians throughout the world. In Israel, these are centred around events in the life of Jesus, such as the Church of the Nativity on Bethlehem and the Church of the Holy Sepulchre, built over the tomb where his body lay.

In other parts of the world Christians visit scenes of visions and miracles. Lourdes in France is an example of this and is now regarded by many as a place of healing. Roman Catholics make a special point of visiting Rome, not only for its historical significance in the development of Christianity, but also because it is the home of the Pope.

Festivals

The Church year begins on 30 November, St Andrew's Day, and is followed by celebrations of the main events in Jesus's life.

- Advent – 24 days leading up to birth of Jesus; Christians use this as a time of preparation and remember the visit of the angel to Mary.
- Christmas – a joyful festival when Christians give thanks for Jesus's birth.
- Epiphany – the visit of the wise men to Jesus at his birth; it is celebrated as Christmas by Orthodox Christians; it also remembers Jesus's baptism.
- Lent – the time following his baptism when Jesus prepared for his ministry; Christians use this as a special time of penitence to get ready for the holiest part of the year.
- Easter – Jesus's death and resurrection, events central to Christianity.
- Ascension – the time when Jesus returned to Heaven.
- Whitsun – a traditional time of baptism when Christians remember the giving of the Holy Spirit and the beginning of the Church.
- Trinity – the rest of the year when Christians recall Jesus's ministry and teaching.
- Saints days are also celebrated by different denominations during the year.

What's it all about?

After Jesus's death, the disciples formed communities that became known as 'churches'; this did not refer to buildings but to the people themselves.

Followers became known as Christians and they met together in their houses to remember Jesus and his message.

These churches kept in touch by letters, 21 of which remain in the New Testament.

By 65 CE the persecution of Christians had begun but rather than wipe the religion out it helped the faith to spread throughout the Roman Empire and beyond.

In 412 CE, under the Emperor Constantine, Christianity became accepted and later became the religion of the Roman Empire. Missionaries were sent to other countries carrying the message.

From 1054 CE, the Church began to divide into different groups; today the main divisions are Orthodox, Roman Catholic and Protestant. The Protestant Church is made up of a variety of denominations. These all follow the same basic beliefs as those above but choose to worship in different ways. Today the Ecumenical Movement seeks to unite the churches rather than stress the differences.

What do Christians believe?

Roman Catholics accept and follow the teachings of the Pope, believed to be the direct successor to the Apostle, Peter, who is regarded as the first Bishop of Rome. The Orthodox and Protestant Churches take their authority from the Bible as the word of God.

The main beliefs of Christians are set out in the Apostles' Creed (from the Latin 'credo' meaning 'I believe'). This is a prayer based on the early teachings of the Apostles.

These include:

- Belief in the Trinity, an idea to explain how three persons make up one God – God the Father, God the Son and God the Holy Spirit.
- Belief that God the Father is the creator and father of all things.
- Belief that God the Son is Jesus Christ, born to a virgin called Mary; he lived on earth and was crucified, died and was buried and rose again three days later. He now reigns in Heaven with God the Father and will return to judge the living and the dead.
- Belief that God as the Holy Spirit is God's power and inspiration in a person's life and this was given to Jesus's disciples after he had returned to Heaven.
- Belief in the catholic church. In this sense, the word 'catholic' means 'universal' or 'worldwide' and the word 'church' refers to all the Christians who form part of this fellowship throughout the world.
- Belief in the 'communion of saints', referring to the relationship between all Christians, alive as well as dead.
- Christians believe that anyone who is truly sorry for what they have done wrong can be forgiven by God providing they are sincerely determined not to repeat the sin.
- Belief that there is life after death for all believers.

Famous twentieth-century Christians

Martin Luther King (1929–68) worked for Civil Rights in America through non-violent protests.

Desmond Tutu (1939–present) first black archbishop in South Africa who chaired the Truth and Reconciliation Committee following the end of Apartheid.

Mother Teresa (1910–1997) worked with the poor and dying on the streets of Calcutta, India.

Christianity today has spread throughout the world and is the principle religion of many countries.

Islam key facts

Islam – what is it?

Where and when did it begin?
In Arabia during the early seventh century CE.

Who founded it?
The Prophet Muhammad (pbuh) who lived 570–633 CE.

Special writings
The Qur'an is the basic source of all Islamic teachings and laws.

The Hadith – the teachings, sayings and actions of the Prophet Muhammad (pbuh) recorded and collected by his devoted companions – explain the Qur'anic verses.

Symbol
A crescent moon.

Places of worship
Muslims can practise their religion anywhere, but especially at home or in a mosque.

Pilgrimages
The Hajj to Makkah (also spelt Mecca) leads to the Ka'bah built by the Prophet Abraham over 3,000 years ago. Jerusalem is also considered a Muslim holy city.

Festivals
The most important event in the Muslim calendar is Ramadan (the ninth month of the Islamic year) – a holy month of fasting. The beginning of the next month (Id-ul-Fitr) is a time of celebration when people give money to the poor (zakah).

What's it all about?

Muhammad (pbuh)
The Prophet Muhammad (pbuh) was born in Makkah, Arabia. He came from a noble family, led a perfect life and set an example to those around him. At the age of 40, while meditating in the Cave of Hira, he received his first revelation from God through the angel Jibra'il. For the next 23 years Muhammad's (pbuh) revelations continued and he preached his message across Arabia. His revelations were written down by scribes and formed the Islamic holy book, the Qur'an. Although he and his followers were persecuted and had to face severe hardships, they finally converted the pagan city of Makkah into the centre of the Muslim faith. Within a century of Muhammad's (pbuh) death Islam had spread from Spain in the west to China in the east.

What do Muslims believe?

'Submission to the will of God'. This word comes from the same root as the Arabic word 'salam' which means 'peace'. The religion of Islam is the surrender to the 'will of Allah' – the complete acceptance of the teachings and guidance of God. The faith believes in the one God who created the universe. Throughout the world Muslims prefer to use the Arabic word 'Allah' for 'God'. They believe that every action done with the awareness that it fulfils the 'will of Allah' is an act of worship. Nevertheless the following specific acts of worship, called the 'Pillars of Islam', make up the basic framework of daily life:

Where is Islam practised?

Islam began in its present form 1400 years ago in Arabia but quickly spread to become a global religion. Today there are over 1.2 billion Muslims worldwide with around 2 million Muslims in Britain. The countries with the largest Islamic populations are in Asia, particularly Indonesia, Pakistan, Bangladesh and India.

Islam is a religion for all people whatever race or background they might be. Muslims are to be found on every continent in the world and Islam is the main religion in Afghanistan, Malaysia, Azerbaijan, Turkmenistan, Uzbekistan, Iran, Iraq, Syria, Jordan, the Arab States, and Turkey and in Africa in Egypt, Algeria, Tunisia, Djibouti, Gambia, Guinea, Libya, Mali, Mauritanian, Morocco, Niger, Somalia, Senegal, Sudan and Zanzibar. Large Muslim communities are also to be found in Europe, particularly Albania, Bosnia and Macedonia, elsewhere in Europe immigrant communities of Muslims exist. In the Americas the Islamic population has greatly increased in recent years both from conversions and the immigration of Muslims from other parts of the world.

Pillars of Islam

1 The declaration of faith
'I bear witness that there is none worthy of worship except Allah and that Muhammad (pbuh) is His servant and messenger'; the prophethood of Muhammad (pbuh) obliges individual Muslims to follow his example in every way.

2 Prayer
Muslims must pray five times daily: at dawn, at noon, in the mid-afternoon, at dusk, and after dark. The world, according to Islam, is a place of trial and we are being judged in it. Prayer purifies the heart, strengthens faith and helps control any temptation to do wrong.

3 Zakah
Muslims must pay a percentage of their earnings to help the poor and needy. This is called zakah. It shows that everything we possess belongs to Allah and therefore anyone in need has a share in it.

4 Fasting
Once each year, during the month of Ramadan, Muslims observe the fast. From dawn to sunset Muslims must not eat, drink, smoke or have intimate marital relationships. Fasting is much more than not eating or drinking but a period of total physical and emotional cleansing when a Muslim struggles against all evil thoughts and desires. (jihad)

5 Hajj
Muslims try to go on Hajj at least once in a lifetime provided they have the means to do so. Hajj requires that people temporarily put their normal daily lives on hold and together with millions of other pilgrims of all races and nations a Muslim has an opportunity to stand in front of Allah alone.

How is Islam different?
Islam is not a new religion. It contains, in essence, the same message and guidance revealed to the prophets Abraham, Moses and Jesus. Muslims believe that the message revealed to Muhammad (pbuh), the last Prophet, is Islam in its complete and final form. In Islam there is no hierarchy of priests or complicated rituals. Everybody may read and learn from the Qur'an directly and put its teachings into use in everyday life.

Judaism key facts

Judaism – what is it?

Where and when did it begin?

Judaism is the religion of the Jews and it began over 3000 years ago at the time of Abraham when God made an agreement with him. This agreement or covenant, was that God would look after his people, keep them safe.

Special writings

The Hebrew Bible is made up of many books. The Torah, the first five books of the Bible, contains the teachings. These are considered to be very important because it tells Jewish people how they should live their lives, it gives them rules they should follow. The Neviim tells of the Prophets and their lives, how God spoke through them. The Ketuvim are writings that glorify God and are often used in worship.

Torah

Genesis
Exodus
Leviticus
Numbers
Deuteronomy

Neviim	Ketuvim
Joshua	Psalms
Judges	Proverbs
1 and 2 Samuel	Job
1 and 2 Kings	Song of Songs
Isaiah	Ruth
Jeremiah	Lamentations
Ezekiel	Ecclesiastes
Hosea	Esther
Joel	Ruth
Amos	Daniel
Obadiah	Ezra
Jonah	Nehemiah
Micah	1 and 2
Nahum	Chronicles
Habbakuk	
Zephaniah	
Haggai	
Zechariah	
Malachai	

You may recognize some of these books as forming part of the Old Testament in the Bible. For Jews these are not a part of the Old Testament; they are part of their holy Bible and show God's promise to them.

Another important holy book is the Talmud. This contains the ideas and teachings of great Jewish scholars and is often referred to when people are unsure about how they should behave in a situation.

Where do Jews worship?

Jews worship in a synagogue, the word literally means meeting place, and it is a focal point of the Jewish community. Synagogues are always built facing toward Jerusalem because this is where Solomon built his Temple before it was destroyed and the Jews were forced to leave their homeland and live in Babylon.

The synagogue is not just used as a place of worship, children go there to learn Hebrew and about the Torah. It can be somewhere to meet and talk through problems.

Inside a synagogue you will notice several distinctive features. There may be an area for men to pray and a separate area for women. Some Jews believe that women can distract men from prayer.

You will also notice a cupboard known as the Ark. This is important because in here the Torah scrolls are kept. When the Torah scrolls are not being used they are kept in special covers.

There will also be the bimah. This is a raised platform where the Torah sits during a service; it is higher than everyone else to show that God's word is more important.

Above the Ark you will see a light burning. This light never goes out and represents God looking after his people. He is always with them. Another feature you will notice are two stone tablets. These will have Hebrew writing on them and they represent the ten sayings that God gave to Moses on the top of Mount Sinai.

Also in the synagogue you will see an important Jewish symbol, the Star of David. This represents a shield against evil.

Festivals

Shabbat

This is a weekly celebration remembering God creating the world in six days and resting on the seventh. It begins at sunset on Friday and ends twenty five hours later. Traditionally Jews stop working for the whole day; it is a day of rest.

Rosh Hashanah and Yom Kippur

This marks the New Year for Jews and is a time when they think about the things they have done wrong; they say sorry and ask for forgiveness from God at Yom Kippur, the Day of Atonement. On this day Jews will fast and pray.

Sukkot

This is a festival about thanking God for all the things He has given his people.

Simchat Torah

This is an important celebration for Jews as it marks the beginning of the reading of the Torah in the synagogue. The Jews thank God for the law that He has given them.

Hannukah

Hannukah lasts for eight days at the start of December and is known as the Festival of Lights remembering a miracle when Judas defeated the Greek army and reclaimed the Temple for the Jews. Judas and his people threw out all the Greek idols and looked to relight the Menorah, the seven-headed candle. This light in the Temple was never allowed to go out but there was only enough oil for it to keep burning for one day. However, the light stayed alight whilst the Jews waited for more oil to arrive in Jerusalem.

Purim

This celebration remembers how good will overcome evil and the bravery of Esther, who, through careful planning and with God's help, saved the Jewish people from death.

Pesach

This festival, often referred to as Passover, remembers how God saved his people from the Egyptians, and how his people wandered for 40 years in the desert before claiming the promised land. This festival remembers God's power as He caused the ten plagues which led to the Exodus of the Israelites from Egypt.

Shavuot

This celebration remembers how Moses was given the Law by God.

What do Jews believe?

Jewish belief is captured in the Shema, a statement of faith that is said each morning and each evening. This can be found in Deuteronomy 6:4–5.

'Hear O Israel! The Lord is our God, the Lord is one! And you shall love the Lord your God with all your heart and with all your soul and with all your might.'

This is written on a piece of parchment and can be found in a mezuzah, nailed to the doorpost of a Jewish home and outside each room except the bathroom. Whenever a Jew enters a room they will touch the mezuzah to remind themselves of the Shema.

For Jews, God is everywhere. He created the world and can act within the world to help His people.

They follow the Ten Commandments found in Exodus 20:1–17, and other laws known as the mitzvot.

Jewish people follow strict laws about food. They have foods that are kosher, or permitted, and non-kosher foods – food which should not be eaten.

Foods that are kosher are:

- Fish that have fins and scales such as cod.
- Animals that have cloven hooves and eat grass.
- Birds such as chicken; birds of prey are not allowed.

Buddhism key facts

Buddhism – what is it?

Where and when did it begin?
Buddhism began in India about 2500 years ago.

Who founded it?
The Buddha, who lived 563–483 BCE.

Special writings
There are several types of Buddhism, each of which have different texts. Two very important ones are: 'The Pali Canon' and 'The Perfection of Wisdom'. Both are very long and describe the Buddha's life story, how to be a Buddhist, and what the truth about life really is.

Symbol
An eight-spoked wheel.

Places of worship
Buddhists can practise their religion anywhere, but especially at home or in temples. Monks live in 'viharas' or monasteries.

Pilgrimages
Buddhists might go on pilgrimages to many special places, but four are particularly important: where the Buddha was born, became enlightened, taught his first sermon, and died.

Festivals
Buddhist festivals can differ from country to country. However, one major festival that all Buddhists celebrate is on the full moon in May. It marks three occasions in the Buddha's life – his birth, enlightenment and death.

What's it all about?

The Buddha
Siddhartha Gautama was born into a very wealthy family, but as he grew older he realized that his great fortune would never stop him suffering from old age, sickness and death. At 29 he decided to leave all of his luxury and his family behind, and set out to see if there was a solution to these sufferings that all human beings face. For six years he learned all he could from many great teachers, but even they could not give him a solution. Eventually he sat down under a tree in Bodh Gaya (in North India), and meditated all night. By morning he had understood the deepest truths about life, and he was free from ever having to suffer again; he had become 'enlightened'. From this point on he became known as 'the Buddha' which means 'one who is fully awake' to the truth. For the next 45 years he taught other people how to become enlightened and free themselves from suffering. He died at the age of 80 leaving others to carry on his teachings.

What do Buddhists believe?

Buddhists believe that the Buddha had found a solution to life's sufferings, and that if they follow his teachings they can help themselves – and others – to find perfect peace and happiness. Buddhists call Buddhism 'the dharma' which means 'the truth' or 'law' about the way things really are. The Buddha summarized his teachings in 'The Four Noble Truths':

1 Life always involves suffering of some sort. Even when we feel happy, it never seems to last.

2 The cause of this suffering is our own ignorance or 'wrong-thinking' about ourselves. We should recognize that our own minds are full of wrong ideas, and, because of them we end up being driven by desires that stop us from realizing the truth.

3 However, the cause of this suffering – our ignorance and desires – can be 'blown out' ('nirvana') by realizing the truth. We can then be free from all suffering, and be perfectly happy and peaceful.

4 We can achieve nirvana by perfecting eight special skills or 'following the Eight Fold Path'. (That is why there are eight spokes in the Buddhist symbol – eight skills that free you from the 'wheel of life').

The eight special skills involve:

- Morality – learning how to act in a good way (good karma) and avoid bad actions (bad karma). This includes being kind, non-violent and honest to everyone, for example

- Wisdom – working hard to understand Buddhist teachings about the truth of life. This includes studying the words of the Buddha and seeing how they make sense in our own lives

- Meditation – training the mind to be calm and focused, so that we can realize the truth of the Buddhist teachings through direct experience and not just as 'an idea'.

How is Buddhism different?

Buddhism differs from other religions in several ways. It teaches that there is no God, no 'unchanging soul', and that the way to find deep and true happiness is *our own responsibility*. The Buddha is seen as a very special man, but he is not regarded as 'being alive today' by most Buddhists. His image in temples is often used as an inspiration or a focus for meditation. However, it is important to realize that there are many kinds of Buddhists, and that they might have different views about what their religion teaches and how it might be practised.

Where is Buddhism practised?
Buddhism began in India, but spread to many other countries over the centuries, particularly in Asia. Tibet, Mongolia, Thailand, Laos, Vietnam, Sri Lanka are all Buddhist countries today and both Japan and China were heavily influenced by Buddhism in their past. The dharma has also became very popular in the West in the last 50 years; there are Buddhist centres in most European countries and many in America.

Whenever Buddhism moved to another country it met many new influences. These countries would already have their own religions, languages, festivals and traditions. Consequently Buddhism would adapt to fit in with its new surroundings and this explains why there are many different types of Buddhism today. All forms of Buddhism, however, still follow the basic teachings of the Four Noble Truths and the life of the Buddha.

Famous Buddhists: The Dalai Lama
Perhaps the most famous Buddhist in the world is Tenzin Gyatso, the fourteenth Dalai Lama (meaning Ocean of Wisdom). He is a Tibetan Buddhist monk who is regarded as the fourteenth reincarnation of the first Dalai Lama (a great spiritual teacher) who lived 600 years ago. Buddhists all over the world see the fourteenth Dalai Lama as a great example of someone who is kind, compassionate and wise.

The Dalai Lama used to live in Tibet, ruling his huge country (the size of Western Europe) even when he was a teenager. However, when the Chinese invaded Tibet in 1950, the fourteenth Dalai Lama was forced to flee to safety nine years later and he now heads the 'Tibetan Government in Exile' in northern India. Despite all the terrible things that his people have suffered under Chinese rule in Tibet, the Dalai Lama still strongly believes in finding non – violent solutions to the problem. Compassion and ahimsa, or non-violence, are very important parts of Buddhist belief and practise.

Hinduism key facts

Hinduism – what is it?

It is important to realize that there are many ways of believing and worshipping in Hinduism. The religion is grouped around the central beliefs which many Hindus share. For this reason many Hindus prefer their religion to be known 'Sanatan Dharma' (eternal laws or teaching) as they believe this reflects the fact that it is more a way of life than a religion which often reflects the way they eat, whom they marry and even the jobs they do. The Hindu tradition is very diverse. Many Hindus will worship in different ways or consider certain festivals as special.

Where and when did it begin?

Hinduism is one of the world's oldest religions. People were worshipping in the Indus Valley in India over 3000 years ago.

Who founded it?

There was no one founder. There is evidence of its existence over 4500 years ago among the people of the Indus Valley.

Special writings

There are several special writings. Different Hindus consider some writings more important than others. The oldest writings are the Vedas, which contain hymns, stories of gods and goddesses, poetry and religious and social laws. The Upanishads are hymns and poems that discuss questions about life. The Ramayana and the Mahabharata are two special poems. The Bhagavad Gita is an important part of the Mahabharata.

Symbol

The Aum. This is considered to be the first sound at the start of creation.

Places of worship

Although Hindus will often go to the mandirs, or temples, for festivals, most will also worship daily at their own home shrine. Some of the mandirs are very large and elaborate, like Swaminarayan Mandir in Neasden, others are small and simple. Each temple is really a house for its particular god. It is the priest's duty to look after the image of the god (murti) and to treat it like a very special visitor. Worship in the home is important for many Hindus. There will often be a shrine to the family's chosen diety. It may be on a shelf or in the corner of a room. Here the family will perform daily worship or puja.

Pilgrimages

Most of the places of pilgrimage are in India. Varanasi on the River Ganga (also called the Ganges) and the town of Vrindavan where Krishna lived as a child are especially important. The river Ganga is an especially important place for pilgrimage. Many pilgrims go there to spinkle ashes or to say prayers for the dead.

Festivals

There are many Hindu festivals as all the gods have days when they are remembered and worshipped. Not all Hindus celebrate every festival. There are two main reasons for Hindu festivals:

- To celebrate the lives of gods and goddesses.
- To celebrate the seasons.

In Britain most Hindus celebrate Divali, which remembers the story of Rama and Sita. It is often called the festival of lights and can last as long as five days.

The festival of Holi is in the spring and is usually a time for fun. Hindus tell stories of the practical jokes that Krishna played and often throw coloured water at each other.

Raksha Bandhan is often celebrated in August. It is a time when brothers and sisters show their love and affection for each other. They will often exchange gifts including a rakhi (friendship bracelet).

What's it all about?

Hindus believe in one 'Supreme being', or soul, from whom everything comes. This great soul is called Brahman. Brahman is like the root of a tree and everything else in the world is the branches and leaves. There are many different gods or goddesses (deities), which represent different aspects of Brahman's nature and power.

In the temple and home shrine Hindus will often focus their worship on statues of the gods and goddesses. These are called murtis.

What do Hindus believe?

Hindus consider their religion as a way of life. There are duties and codes (dharma), which everyone is expected to follow no matter how young or old. Every person has their own individual soul, or atman. It is this atman that moves through a cycle of birth, death and rebirth and so forms the process of reincarnation.

Since each living being has an atman, many Hindus are vegetarians and consider it wrong to kill an animal, as they are part of the same spirit. The cow is an animal which is considered very special and many Hindus will not eat beef or wear leather.

Hindus believe that how a person is reincarnated depends upon their 'karma'. This is the law of cause and effect. Hindus believe that whatever they do their actions will have a result in the future. The aim of a Hindu's life is to break free of this endless chain of birth, death and rebirth to achieve 'moksha' where the atman becomes one with Brahman.

The Bhagavad Gita tells of three pathways to follow which will lead to this aim:

1 Knowledge – to study the special books of Hinduism and to think deeply about their teachings.

2 Yoga – to carry out exercises for the mind and the body.

3 Bhakti – to show a love for God through prayer and service.

Famous twentieth century Hindus

Mahatma Gandhi (1869–1948) was a political and religious leader in India. In his campaign for fair treatment and equality he always used non-violent actions. His peaceful approach and words have been a major influence on many twentieth-century Hindus and non-Hindus.

Sikhism key facts

Sikhism – what is it?

Where and when did it begin?
Sikhism began in India in the fifteenth century CE.

Who founded it?
Guru Nanak Dev Ji, who lived 1469–1539 CE (guru means teacher).

Special writings
The main book for Sikhs is called the Guru Granth Sahib Ji. It contains the teachings of Guru Nanak Dev Ji and the nine gurus who followed after him.

Symbol
The Khanda.

Places of worship
Sikhs worship in the home and in a building called a gurdwara. The word gurdwara means 'doorway to the guru'. Every gurdwara has a langar. This is a kitchen that serves free food.

Pilgrimages
A special place for Sikhs is Amritsar, in the Punjab in India. Guru Arjan Dev Ji built what is known as the Golden Temple. It is where the Guru Granth Sahib Ji is kept.

Festivals
Sikhs have many festivals. They include Divali, celebrating the festival of light; Baisakhi, which celebrates the forming of the Khalsa (Sikh community); and gurpurbs, which are festivals that remember the gurus.

What's it all about?

Guru Nanak Dev Ji was brought up as a Hindu. However as he grew up he was influenced by both Hinduism and Islam and became discontented with the beliefs and practices of these two religions. It is believed that one day Guru Nanak Dev Ji went to bathe in a river and disappeared. He was said to have drowned, but after three days he miraculously returned. Guru Nanak Dev Ji claimed that he met with God who revealed to him that there was no difference between Hindus and Muslims; all people belong to God.

Guru Nanak Dev Ji travelled around spreading his teachings. Nine gurus followed after him and continued to spread his message:

1　Guru Angad Dev Ji (1504–52) – he translated the hymns of Guru Nanak into a language called Gurmukhi.

2　Guru Amar Das Ji (1479–1574) – he spread many teachings of Sikhism. He developed the idea of the langar.

3　Guru Ram Das Ji (1534–81) – he founded the city of Amritsar.

4　Guru Arjan Dev Ji (1563–1606) – he was the first Sikh martyr (someone who dies for their beliefs). He collected together the teachings of the gurus and built the Golden Temple at Amritsar.

5　Guru Har Gobind Ji (1595–1644) – he trained Sikhs to fight so they could defend their faith.

6　Guru Hari Rai Ji (1630–61) – he worked towards spreading peace. He is remembered for his caring and generous nature.

7　Guru Hari Krishan Ji (1656–64) – he died as a child.

8　Guru Tegh Behadur Ji (1621–1675) – he was the second Sikh martyr.

9　Guru Gobind Singh Ji (1666–1708) – he completed the Guru Granth Sahib Ji and started the community of Sikhs (the Khalsa).

Eventually, all of the teachings of the ten gurus were recorded in the Guru Granth Sahib Ji.

What do Sikhs believe?

The Mool Mantar is the basic statement of belief for Sikhs. It states that there is one God (Il Onkar) and that He has no beginning or end. He is the creator and is all-loving.

Sikhs believe in reincarnation. They believe that when they die the soul lives on and is continually reborn. The aim of life is to break free from being reborn and to be united with God.

Sikhs wear five objects, called the Five Ks, which demonstrate their beliefs. Each object begins with the letter 'K' in Punjabi:

1　**Kachera** – shorts, originally these represented freedom to move when in battle defending the faith.

2　**Kara** – a steel bracelet, symbolic of the fact that God has no beginning or end.

3　**Kesh** – uncut hair. Hair is a gift from God; it is left uncut to show devotion to Him.

4　**Kirpan** – a short sword, symbolic of a Sikh's duty to defend his or her faith.

5　**Kangha** – a wooden comb, used by Sikhs to keep their hair in good condition.

Sikhs believe that all religions are pathways to the one God. They reject the belief that it is right to worship idols (false gods).

Sikhism in the twentieth century

Sikhism originally started in the Punjab in India. Today many Sikhs live in Britain and all over the world. Many people from India, including Sikhs, came to Britain in the 1950s at the invitation of the British government to work due to a labour shortage and the need to rebuild the industry after the Second World War.

Another factor that influenced the movement of Sikhs to Britain was the events of 1947. Up until then India had been part of the British Empire, but in 1947 India became independent and was split into two countries, Pakistan and India. The Sikh home of the Punjab was split right down the middle. Many Sikhs were unhappy with this decision and it resulted in some of them leaving the Punjab. Despite the distance most Sikhs still regard Amritsar as their spiritual home.

Index

Index

Themes in RE:
Learning from Religions

The stimulating issues-based course that raises students' performance

This series for Key Stage 3 explores the major religions through contemporary and relevant themes. Specifically designed to challenge your students' understanding in RE, it provides an ideal grounding for issues-based studies at Key Stage 4.

➤ The three Student Books, suitable for each year of the Key Stage, create a natural progression of your students' skills through recurring themes.

➤ The accompanying Teacher's Resource Files contain photocopiable sheets, suggestions for homework and help on assessment and evaluation, so you can accurately monitor your students' progress.

➤ The series examines six themes across the major world faiths, encouraging your students to learn *both* about and *from* religions.

Themes in RE: Learning from Religions	
Student Book 1 0 435 30750 9	**Teacher's Resource File 1** 0 435 30752 5
Student Book 2 0 435 30766 5	**Teacher's Resource File 2** 0 435 30768 1
Student Book 3 0 435 30786 X	**Teacher's Resource File 3** 0 435 30788 6

Heinemann

tel **01865 888068**   *fax* **01865 314029**   *email* **orders@heinemann.co.uk**   *web* **www.heinemann.co.uk**